Developing Ideas

Intro

EFFECTIVE
Academic Writing

SECOND EDITION

Alice Savage

OXFORD
UNIVERSITY PRESS

OXFORD
UNIVERSITY PRESS

198 Madison Avenue
New York, NY 10016 USA

Great Clarendon Street, Oxford, OX2 6DP, United Kingdom

Oxford University Press is a department of the University of Oxford.
It furthers the University's objective of excellence in research, scholarship,
and education by publishing worldwide. Oxford is a registered trade
mark of Oxford University Press in the UK and in certain other countries

General Manager, American ELT: Laura Pearson
Publisher: Stephanie Karras
Associate Publishing Manager: Sharon Sargent
Managing Editor: Jennifer Meldrum
Director, ADP: Susan Sanguily
Executive Design Manager: Maj-Britt Hagsted
Associate Design Manager: Michael Steinhofer
Image Manager: Trisha Masterson
Electronic Production Manager: Julie Armstrong
Production Artist: Elissa Santos
Production Coordinator: Chris Espejo
Production Coordinator: Brad Tucker

ISBN: 978 0 19 432345 1 EFFECTIVE ACADEMIC WRITING INTRO WITH ONLINE
PRACTICE PACK
ISBN: 978 0 19 432344 4 EFFECTIVE ACADEMIC WRITING INTRO STUDENT BOOK AS
PACK COMPONENT
ISBN: 978 0 19 433391 7 EFFECTIVE ACADEMIC WRITING ONLINE

Printed in China

This book is printed on paper from certified and well-managed sources

ACKNOWLEDGEMENTS

*The authors and publisher are grateful to those who have given permission to reproduce
the following extracts and adaptations of copyright material:*

p. 109 From *To Kill a Mocking Bird* by Harper Lee. Copyright © 1960 by Harper
Lee; renewed © 1988 by Harper Lee. Foreward copyright 1993 by Harper Lee.
Reprinted by permission of HarperCollins Publishers.

Illustrations by: p. 25 Joe Taylor; p. 37 Barb Bastian.

*We would also like to thank the following for permission to reproduce the following
photographs:*

Cover, Joao Paulo/Getty Images; p. viii, Marcin Krygier / iStockphoto (laptop);
p. vi, Opener, Writing Process and Review pages, 159 stocksnapper/
istockphoto (letter texture); pp. 33, 51, 69, 87, 105, 123, 141 Monkey Business
Images/Shutterstock (Clock); p. 1 iStockphoto/Thinkstock; p. 2 Ingram
Publishing/Thinkstock (writing); p. 2 Tetra Images/Alamy (marking);
p. 2 iStockphoto/Thinkstock (reading); p. 17 Viviane Moos/Corbis UK Ltd.;
p. 18 Viviane Moos/Corbis UK Ltd.; p. 21 UpperCut/Oxford University Press
(gallery); p. 21 Robert Harding Picture Library Ltd/Alamy (plaza); p. 21 Maria
Galan/Alamy (stadium); p. 21 MARKA /Alamy (beach); p. 35 Image Source/
Oxford University Press; p. 36 Goodshoot/Thinkstock (sunglasses);
p. 36 Image Source/Oxford University Press(spectacles); p. 40 iStockphoto/
Thinkstock (backpack); p. 40 Africa Studio/Shutterstock (purse);
p. 43 Shebeko/Shutterstock (necklace); p. 43 Igor Grochev/Shutterstock
(watch); p. 43 mike stone/Oxford University Press (boots); p. 53 Peter Menzel/
Science Photo Library; p. 54 Liz Boyd/Oxford University Press (Asimo);
p. 54 Peter Menzel/Science Photo Library (RHcx robot); p. 71 Michele Falzone/
Alamy; p. 72 Michele Falzone/Alamy; p. 89 Justin Kase/Alamy; p. 90 Justin
Kase/Alamy; p. 103 Steppenwolf/Alamy; p. 107 JTavin/Everett/Rex Features;
p. 108 JTavin/Everett/Rex Features; p. 125 David Lichtneker/Alamy;
p. 126 David Lichtneker/Alamy.

Reviewers

We would like to acknowledge the following individuals for their input during the development of the series:

Chris Alexis, College of Applied Sciences, Sur, Oman

Amina Saif Mohammed Al Hashamia, College of Applied Sciences, Nizwa, Oman

Amal Al Muqarshi, College of Applied Sciences, Ibri, Oman

Saleh Khalfan Issa Al-Rahbi, College of Applied Sciences, Nizwa, Oman

Dr. Debra Baldwin, UPP, Alfaisal University, Saudi Arabia

Virginia L. Bouchard, George Mason University, English Language Institute, Washington D.C.

Judith Buckman, College of Applied Sciences, Salalah, Oman

Dr. Catherine Buon, American University of Armenia, Armenia

Mei-Rong Alice Chen, National Taiwan University of Science and Technology, Taipei

Mark L. Cummings, Jefferson Community and Technical College, KY

Hitoshi Eguchi, Hokusei Gakuen University, Japan

Elizabeth W. Foss, Washtenaw Community College, MI

Sally C. Gearhart, Santa Rosa Junior College, CA

Alyona Gorokhova, Miramar Community College, CA

Dr. Simon Green, College of Applied Sciences, Oman

Janis Hearn, Hongik University, South Korea

Adam Henricksen, University of Maryland, Baltimore County, MD

Clay Hindman, Sierra College, CA

Kuei-ping Vicky Hsu, National Tsing Hua University, Hsinchu

Azade Johnson, Abu Dhabi Men's College, Higher Colleges of Technology, U.A.E.

Chandra Johnson, Fresno Pacific University, CA

Pei-Lun Kao, Chang Gung University, Gueishan

Yuko Kobayashi, Tokyo University of Science, Japan

Blair Lee, Kyung Hee University, Japan

Chia-yu Lin, National Tsing Hua University, Hsinchu

Kent McClintock, Chosun University, South Korea

Joan Oakley, College of the North Atlantic-Qatar, Qatar

Fernanda G. Ortiz, CESL University of Arizona, AZ

William D. Phelps, Southern Illinois University, IL

Dorothy Ramsay, College of Applied Sciences, Sohar, Oman

Vidya Rangachari, Mission College, CA

Elizabeth Rasmussen, Northern Virginia Community College, VA

Syl Rice, Abu Dhabi Men's College, Higher Colleges of Technology, U.A.E.

Donna Schaeffer, University of Washington, WA

Dr. Catherine Schaff-Stump, Kirkwood Community College, IA

Mary-Jane Scott, Sungshin Women's University, South Korea

Jenay Seymour, Hong-ik University, South Korea

Janet Sloan Rachidi, U.A.E. University, Al Ain, U.A.E.

Bob Studholme, U.A.E. University, Al Ain, U.A.E.

Paula Suzuki, SI-UK Language Centre, Japan

Sabine Thépaut, Intensive English Language Institute, University of North Texas, TX

Shu-Hui Yu, Ling Tung University, Taichung

Author Acknowledgments

I would like to thank OUP's Sharon Sargeant for giving me the opportunity to write a book that I've been thinking about for a long time. Also, thanks to Vicky Aeschbacher for her patient, kind, and exacting editing. We made a good team. Alex Regan and Jennifer Meldrum, thank you for the guidance and support along the way. I am also grateful for my students for giving me smiles and puzzles to solve, and a big hug to my lovely family Masoud, Cyrus, and Kaveh for providing hot tea, love, and encouragement.

Contents

Unit	Academic Focus	Rhetorical Focus	Language and Grammar Focus
6 Explaining Changes page 89	Urban Studies	• Explaining changes with examples	• The present continuous • Spelling rules for the present continuous • Conjunctions • Nouns with *the*
7 Narrating a Past Experience page 107	Psychology	• Narrating a past experience	• Past continuous • Combining past continuous and the simple past • Reporting requests, warnings, and directions with infinitives
8 Explaining Opinions page 125	Health and Wellness	• Explaining an opinion	• Gerunds to describe tasks and activities • *Because* to give reasons • Introducing examples

APPENDICES

Welcome to Effective Academic Writing

Effective Academic Writing, Second Edition instills student confidence and provides the tools necessary for successful academic writing.

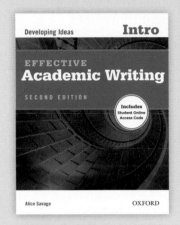

Introductory Level
Developing Ideas

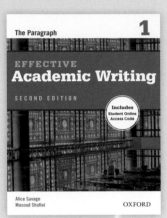

Level 1
The Paragraph

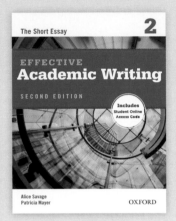

Level 2
The Short Essay

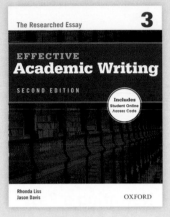

Level 3
The Researched Essay

- Step-by-step **Writing Process** guides and refines writing skills.

- **Timed writing** practice prepares students for success on high-stakes tests.

- **Online Writing Tutor** improves academic writing inside and outside the classroom.

Online Writing Support for all Levels

GO ONLINE

Overview

Effective Academic Writing, Second Edition delivers practice that will improve your students' writing.

- ■ NEW! The new **Introductory Level** provides students with the support and instruction they need for writing success in the lowest-level writing courses.
- ■ NEW! **More content-area related assignments** with more academic vocabulary and readings prepare students for the challenges of the academic classroom.

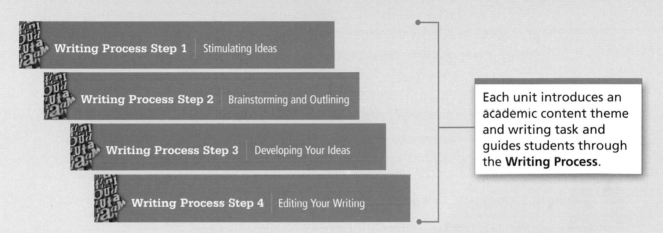

Writing Process Step 1	Stimulating Ideas
Writing Process Step 2	Brainstorming and Outlining
Writing Process Step 3	Developing Your Ideas
Writing Process Step 4	Editing Your Writing

Each unit introduces an academic content theme and writing task and guides students through the **Writing Process**.

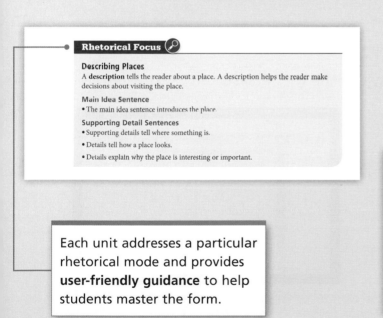

Rhetorical Focus

Describing Places
A **description** tells the reader about a place. A description helps the reader make decisions about visiting the place.

Main Idea Sentence
• The main idea sentence introduces the place.

Supporting Detail Sentences
• Supporting details tell where something is.
• Details tell how a place looks.
• Details explain why the place is interesting or important.

Each unit addresses a particular rhetorical mode and provides **user-friendly guidance** to help students master the form.

Concise and effective language and grammar presentations develop students' understanding and improve their accuracy.

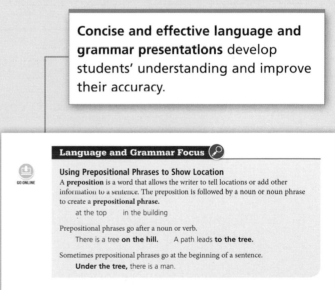

Language and Grammar Focus

GO ONLINE

Using Prepositional Phrases to Show Location
A **preposition** is a word that allows the writer to tell locations or add other information to a sentence. The preposition is followed by a noun or noun phrase to create a **prepositional phrase.**
　　at the top　　in the building

Prepositional phrases go after a noun or verb.
　　There is a tree **on the hill.**　　A path leads **to the tree.**

Sometimes prepositional phrases go at the beginning of a sentence.
　　Under the tree, there is a man.

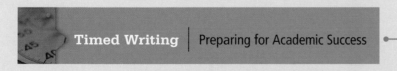

Timed Writing | Preparing for Academic Success

Timed writing prepares students for exams and high-stakes tests.

Effective Academic Writing **Online**

GO ONLINE

IT'S EASY! Use the access code printed on the inside back cover of this book to register at www.effectiveacademicwriting.com.

For the Student

- *Online Writing Tutor* helps students retain and apply their writing skills.

  - Models of the unit writing assignments **demonstrate good writing** and allow students to understand how each text is constructed.
  - **Writing frameworks help students with organizing and structuring,** for the sentence level, paragraph level, and the text as a whole.
  - Students can plan, structure, and write their own texts, check their work, **then save, print, or send directly to their teacher.**

- Extensive **Online Grammar Practice** and **grammar term glossary** support students in using grammar structures appropriately and fluently in their writing.

- Comprehensive **Peer Editor's Checklists** support collaborative learning.

- **Printable Outline Templates** support the writing process.

For the Teacher

- **IELTS-style, TOEFL-style, and TOEIC-style online writing tests** can be **customized** and **printed**.

- **Online test rubrics** make grading easy.

- **Online Grammar Practice** is automatically graded and entered into the online grade book.

- Answer keys make grading easy.

- The **online management system** allows you to manage your classes. View, print, or export all class and student reports.

> **FOR ADDITIONAL SUPPORT**
> Email our customer support team at eltsupport@oup.com.

> **FOR TEACHER CODES**
> Please contact your sales representative for a **Teacher Access Code**. Teacher Access Codes are sold separately.

UNIT 1

Words, Sentences, and Short Paragraphs

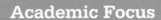

Academic Focus | Writing

Unit Goals

Rhetorical Focus

- main idea sentence and supporting detail sentences
- short paragraphs
- the drafting process

Language and Grammar Focus

- parts of speech
- sentences
- subject and object pronouns

Exercise 1 **Thinking about the topic**

Discuss the pictures with a partner.

- Where are the people in the photos?
- What are they doing?
- What do you think about, talk about, read about, or write about?

Exercise 2 **Reading about the topic**

Read the text below. What do good writers do?

Writers at Work

Good writers have good ideas. Where do those ideas come from? Most writers get ideas from many places. They go for walks. They talk with friends, and they read. In fact, most writers read a lot. Then they are ready to explain their ideas. After they write, they are not finished. They read their work and make changes. They make their ideas clearer. They also check their grammar, spelling, and punctuation. When they finish, their readers will understand and enjoy reading the ideas.

Exercise 3 Understanding the text

Write *T* for true or *F* for false for each statement.

_____ 1. Writers do many things to get ideas.

_____ 2. Talking is not helpful for writing.

_____ 3. Good writers do not need to make changes to their writing.

_____ 4. Writers want people to understand their writing.

Exercise 4 Responding to the text

Answer the following questions about the reading.

1. Where do writers get ideas? _____

   _____

2. Why do writers make changes? _____

   _____

3. What steps do writers follow to write well? _____

   _____

4. What steps do you follow when you write? _____

   _____

Exercise 5 Freewriting

Write for five to ten minutes in your journal. Choose from the topics below or an idea of your own. Don't worry about mistakes.

- What words describe you?
- What is interesting about your life?
- What do you study in school?
- What kind of work do you like?

 In Writing Process Part 2 you will . . .

- learn about words and sentences.

Language and Grammar Focus

Words: Parts of Speech

There are many types of words in English. The most important for vocabulary study are **nouns, verbs,** and **adjectives.**

Nouns name people, places, and things.

person   bridge   nature

Verbs describe actions: things that people do or that happen.

walk   think   break

Adjectives describe nouns.

beautiful   warm   yellow   shy   peaceful

Good writers know how to use nouns, verbs, and adjectives. They choose these words carefully because they want the reader to understand their ideas.

Exercise 1 Identifying nouns

Circle the nouns in the sentences below.

1. (Engineers) designed the (bridge) many (years) ago.
2. Many restaurants serve chicken and potatoes.
3. Trains carry passengers and products.
4. Rice needs a lot of water.
5. Children go to school every day.
6. Many students ride bicycles to school.

Exercise 2 Identifying verbs

Underline the verbs in the sentences below.

1. Managers <u>organize</u> people.
2. A plant needs sunlight.
3. Canada is producing diamonds now.
4. People walk and ride buses downtown.
5. The president talked to the people.
6. The man acts and sings in movies.

Exercise 3 Identifying adjectives

Circle the adjectives in the sentences below.

1. (Busy) people are often (late).
2. Smart people use big numbers.
3. Sick children often feel hot and tired.
4. Cold tea is a popular drink.
5. The early morning is a nice time to see colorful birds.

GO ONLINE

Language and Grammar Focus

Sentences

A **sentence** is a complete idea. The shortest type of sentence has a noun and a verb. The first noun is called the **subject**.

subject	verb

Birds fly.

subject	verb

People do not fly.

Sentences can also have a noun after the verb. These nouns are called **objects**.

verb	object

Taxis carry **passengers.**

verb	object

A waiter serves **food.**

Longer sentences have more nouns, verbs, adjectives, and other words.

People read and study in the school library.

The young nurse called the busy doctor.

Another type of sentence uses the linking verb *be*.

The fire **is** hot.   They **are** nurses.

Capitalize the first letter of the first word in a sentence. End each sentence with a **period**.

x small cars use less gas (incorrect)   Small cars use less gas. (correct)

Exercise 4 Practicing with sentences

Unscramble the sentences below. Remember to capitalize the first letter.
Then put a period after the last letter. Use a separate piece of paper.

1. a phone / the man / has   The man has a phone.
2. busy / the streets / are
3. the woman / an umbrella / carries
4. a raincoat / does not have / the man
5. red / is / the stoplight

Exercise 5 Practicing with punctuation and capitalization

**Read the sentences below. Put a period after each sentence. Change the
first letter of the second sentence to a capital letter.**

1. City buses are important. ᵀthey carry many people.

2. Healthy people eat fruits vegetables are also healthy

3. In tall buildings, people do not use stairs they use elevators

4. Rivers have freshwater the ocean has saltwater

5. Some people like to use texting other people like to talk on the phone

Exercise 6 Identifying complete sentences

**Put a check (✓) next to each sentence that expresses a complete idea. If the
sentence is not a complete idea, correct it.**

_____ 1. They
         ∧ have a big car.   _____ 4. was a computer expert.

_____ 2. Tokyo is busy.   _____ 5. Taxi drivers too fast.

_____ 3. teaches science.   _____ 6. The store very expensive.

 In **Writing Process Part 3** you will . . .

- learn about main idea and supporting detail sentences.
- learn about short paragraphs.
- learn to write first drafts.

Rhetorical Focus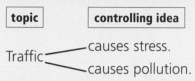

Main Idea Sentence and Supporting Detail Sentences

Good writers organize their ideas. They write a **main idea sentence**. Then they use **supporting details** to explain the main idea.

Main idea sentences have two parts. They have a **topic**. They also have a **controlling idea**. The controlling idea tells what the writer will explain about the topic.

topic	controlling idea

Traffic — causes stress.
Traffic — causes pollution.

Supporting detail sentences give specific information and examples that explain the main idea sentence.

main idea sentence	supporting detail sentence

Bicycles are useful. People can ride them to work.

main idea sentence	supporting detail sentence

Traffic causes stress. People cannot drive fast. They are late to places.

Exercise 1 Creating main idea sentences

Write the letter of the controlling idea next to the topic it supports.

Topics	Controlling Ideas
_d_ 1. Math	a. is hot in the day and cold at night.
____ 2. The desert	b. need a lot of security.
____ 3. Tea	c. can learn many languages at once.
____ 4. Banks	d. is important in engineering work.
____ 5. Children	e. costs a lot of money.
____ 6. A good car	f. is medicine in some countries.

Exercise 2 Identifying main idea and supporting detail sentences

Write *MI* for main idea sentences. Write *SD* for supporting detail sentences.

_MI_ 1. a. There are many different types of doctors.

_SD_   b. Some doctors study the heart; other doctors study the brain.

_____ 2. a. Safety is important to parents.

_____   b. Parents spend 500 million dollars each year on children's safety products.

_____ 3. a. Fish is low in fat and has a lot of vitamins.

_____   b. Fish is healthy.

_____ 4. a. The Internet changed shopping habits.

_____   b. People started to buy products online.

_____ 5. a. Trees add color and attract song birds.

_____   b. Trees are good for a city.

Exercise 3 Practicing with supporting detail sentences

Complete the supporting detail sentences with your own words.

1. Students try to save money. Many students _share an apartment._ _____

2. Construction workers need eye protection. They wear _____

3. Trees are different from bushes. Trees _____

4. Cities are noisy. They have _____

5. Chicken is easy to cook. Many cooks _____

Rhetorical Focus

Short Paragraphs

Main idea sentences often have several supporting details. When this happens, they become **short paragraphs.** A short paragraph follows these rules.

- It starts five spaces inside a margin. This is called **indenting**.
- It has a main idea sentence.
- It has several supporting detail sentences.
- All the sentences follow one another. They do not start on a new line.

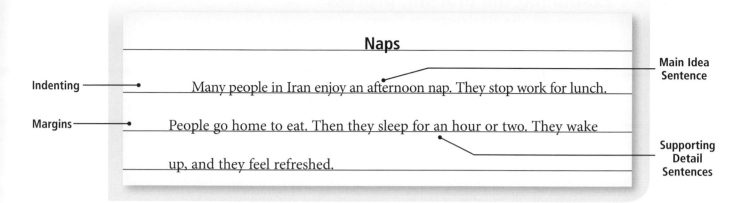

Naps

Indenting

Many people in Iran enjoy an afternoon nap. They stop work for lunch.

Margins

People go home to eat. Then they sleep for an hour or two. They wake

up, and they feel refreshed.

Main Idea Sentence

Supporting Detail Sentences

Exercise 4 Examining a short paragraph

Read the short paragraph, and answer the questions on a separate piece of paper.

Honesty

I always tell the truth. For example, sometimes I am late. I say the

real reason. Also, I sometimes forget birthdays. I tell people I forgot.

1. What is the main idea sentence about?
2. How many supporting detail sentences are there?
3. What do you think about the writer's ideas? Do you believe her? Why or why not?

Rhetorical Focus

Writing a First Draft

Writers write a **first draft** to put their ideas on paper. They know they can make changes later. To write a first draft, follow two steps:

- Write all your ideas as well as you can.

- When you finish, read your work, and make notes. You can add information, change it, or take away information that is not necessary.

About Me

Change

athletic
I am strong. I like sports. Sports are important to me. I play soccer

and tennis. I also ride my bicycle.

Take away unnecessary information

A. Work with a partner. Read the drafts below. Circle the letter of the draft that gives you the best information (the revision).

1. a. Nurses are good. They bring things. They talk. They say kind words. The words are nice.

   b. Nurses help patients. They bring medicine. They answer questions. They say kind words to the patient.

2. a. A tree hurt my relative. The sun was hot. She was under the tree. My cousins were in the water. A thing fell on her. She got hurt.

   b. We were at the beach. The sun was hot. My aunt was in the shade under a tree. A coconut hit her head. She got hurt and went to the hospital. Now she is okay.

3. a. A big family is noisy. Young children play loudly. Sometimes they cry. Older children talk on cell phones or watch television. Mothers make noise with pots and pans.

   b. A family is different. They play. They watch television, and talk too much. There are papers and toys everywhere. Parents work or do other things.

B. Work with a partner. Circle the revisions in the best draft for each item in A. Which of the following strategies did each writer use in each revision?

a. change vocabulary

b. take away unnecessary information

c. add new information

 In **Writing Process Part 4** you will . . .

- learn to edit for subject and object pronouns.
- learn to write a second draft.

When you edit, you make changes that will improve your writing and correct mistakes.

Rhetorical Focus 🔍

Writing a Second Draft

Good writers write two or more drafts. They want to make their ideas clear, and they want their language to be correct.

After you write your draft and your ideas are clear, make sure the language is correct. Check your grammar, spelling, and punctuation to correct mistakes.

M   has
mexico ~~have~~ many parks. *(Capitalize the first letter.)*

Exercise 1 Identifying correct and incorrect sentences

Put a check (✓) next to the correct sentences below. Put an X next to the sentences that are missing a subject, a verb, a capital letter, or a period.

_X_ 1. children go to school.	____ 5. Computers are expensive.
____ 2. Math is easy.	____ 6. Mr. Li teaches science.
____ 3. Students hardworking.	____ 7. The stores close at 8:00.
____ 4. are noisy.	____ 8. The city hot all year.

Exercise 2 Editing practice

Read and edit the main ideas and supporting details below. There are two mistakes in each one.

1. My street is interesting. Many people walk on the street. ^Tthe women carry
   shopping bags. Other people ride bicycles. *The bicycles are* ~~Are~~ different colors.

2. Early morning is a good time to study. it is quiet. I have energy. Have free time
   before school.

3. Older people good leaders. They have experience. help younger people.

4. Rain makes people sad. People in their houses. They do not smile. They quiet

5. A true friend different. A true friend brings happiness a true friend helps with
   problems. This kind of friend is forever.

Language and Grammar Focus

Nouns and Pronouns: Subject Pronouns

Pronouns take the place of nouns. Writers use a noun to introduce a topic. In later sentences, they use a pronoun to represent the topic.

> noun   pronoun
>
> **Oranges** are delicious. **They** are also healthy.

Subject Pronouns			
I*	**I** think about nature.	We	**We** bought a computer.
You*	**You** need help.	They	**They** are working.
He	**He** is shy.	It	**It** is easy.
She	**She** wants more time.		

* *I* and *you* generally do not replace a noun.

Exercise 3 Practicing with subject pronouns

Underline the subject noun in the first sentence. Replace it with a pronoun in the second sentence.

1. <u>Our parents</u> have a boat. ~~Our parents~~ *They* like to go fishing.

2. My mother is a doctor. My mother works with children.

3. The storms caused problems. The storms flooded the city.

4. My teacher worked in Thailand. My teacher lived in the capital.

5. A businessman travels a lot. A businessman has to meet with customers.

6. My family and I lived in Dubai. Now my family and I live in Chicago.

Language and Grammar Focus

Nouns and Pronouns: Object Pronouns

Object pronouns also take the place of nouns. They follow the verb.

> noun   pronoun
>
> I copied the **words.** Then I memorized **them.**

Object Pronouns			
me	The book changed **me.**	us	History teaches **us** many things.
you*	The guide will show **you.**	them	People use **them.**
him	The manager watched **him.**	it*	Children climb **it.**
her	Customers always ask **her.**		

*Note that *you* and *it* are the same in subject and object position.

Exercise 4 Practicing with object pronouns

Replace the object nouns in the second sentence with object pronouns.

                                                                    them

1. Her parents taught her a lot. She appreciates ~~her parents~~.

2. The news surprised the president. No one had told the president.

3. Smart phones are popular. Many companies sell smart phones.

4. My friends and I talked about the news. It worried my friends and me.

5. A woman asked for directions. A police officer helped the woman.

6. Our team played hard. Unfortunately, the other team beat our team.

Exercise 5 Editing for mistakes with subject and object pronouns

Read and edit the paragraph. There are five more pronoun mistakes.

                                                                   She

My friends and I are busy. Magdalena is a mother. ~~Her~~ has three boys. Them are young. She takes care of they. Andrés is a student. Him is taking three classes this semester. I never see you. He is always in the library. Mauricio and Alejandro have jobs. They work in a bookstore. My family and I have a business. It helps we. We make money, but we work very hard.

Exercise 6 Writing a short paragraph

A. Number the sentences in the correct order. Then rewrite them on a separate piece of paper as a paragraph with a main idea sentence and supporting details.

_____ It gives energy and vitamins.

_____ Fruit is healthy.

_____ It also tastes good.

_____ In every country, people enjoy fruit such as oranges and bananas.

__1__ A good diet has a lot of fruit.

B. Use the editor's checklist below to check your work.

Editor's Checklist

Put a check (✓) as appropriate.

○ 1. Is the paragraph written as a paragraph (not a list of sentences)?

○ 2. Is the first sentence indented?

○ 3. Does every sentence begin with a capital letter?

○ 4. Does every sentence have a subject and a verb?

○ 5. Does every sentence end with a period?

 In **Review** you will . . .

- review parts of speech and simple sentences.
- practice editing for punctuation and capitalization.
- review main idea sentences and supporting detail sentences.

In Putting It All Together you will review what you learned in this unit.

Exercise 1 Practicing with parts of speech

Read the sentences below. Then put the words from the sentences into the correct categories in the chart.

1. Venezuela has white beaches.
2. Students study science.
3. Iceland is cold.
4. New chairs and tables are expensive.
5. Tokyo has tall buildings.
6. Happy people smile.

NOUNS	VERBS	ADJECTIVES
Venezuela beaches	has	white

Exercise 2 Practicing with sentences

Choose words from the boxes below to write simple sentences. Don't forget to capitalize the first letter of the first word and put a period at the end.

SUBJECT NOUNS	VERBS	OBJECT NOUNS
people	help	children
students	study	questions
parents	ask	ideas
writers	have	books

1. Writers have ideas.

2. _____

3. _____

4. _____

Exercise 3 Practicing with capitalization and punctuation

Add periods to each paragraph below. Capitalize the first letter of each sentence.

A.
Dinner is my favorite meal. My mother cooks meat and vegetables she also makes rice the food smells good it tastes good, too

B.
Trees are important. they clean the air trees give shade they provide wood trees are also beautiful

Exercise 4 Practicing with main ideas and supporting details

A. Write *MI* next to the main idea sentence. Write *SD* next to the supporting detail sentences.

_SD_ 1. a. Computers are also important for entertainment and work.
_MI_   b. Computers are useful.
_SD_   c. People use them for communication.

_____ 2. a. They also get energy from gas and coal.
_____   b. There are many kinds of energy.
_____   c. People get energy from wind, water, and the sun.

_____ 3. a. Business people travel a lot.
_____   b. They meet customers.
_____   c. They open new markets.

_____ 4. a. Many classrooms have wireless technology.
_____   b. Many students use electronic tablets.
_____   c. Education is changing.

_____ 5. a. They give the correct medicine.
_____   b. They check patients' health.
_____   c. Nurses are careful.

_____ 6. a. Many people work in hotels.
_____   b. Desk clerks check in guests.
_____   c. Housekeepers clean rooms.

B. Choose one of the items in part A, and write it as a paragraph. Use a separate piece of paper. Then use the editing checklist on page 14 to correct any mistakes.

UNIT 2

Describing Places

Unit Goals

Rhetorical Focus

- describing places

Language and Grammar Focus

- prepositions and prepositional phrases
- article *a* or *an*
- singular nouns with *there is*
- plural nouns with *there are*

In this unit, you will describe a tourist attraction.

Exercise 1 Thinking about the topic

Discuss the picture with a partner.

- Where are the people in the picture?
- What do you see?
- What is above them?
- What is next to them?
- Have you ever seen a place like this? Where was it?

Exercise 2 Reading about the topic

A travel writer wants to share the excitement of Times Square in New York City. What does she think is the most important attraction?

Times Square

To experience Times Square in New York, you must go there. It is not the buildings or even the big digital **billboards** that make it special. It is the movement. On a typical day, New Yorkers are everywhere, and they are moving fast. There are rich ladies wearing diamond jewelry. There is a street **musician** playing an **accordion.** Tourists take pictures of each other in front of theaters. A taxi pulls over, and an **elegant** couple in traditional African dress get out. A famous actor walks into the street to get away from fans. He disappears into the crowd. You look up and see his face on a billboard.

billboards: large outdoor advertisements
musician: a person who plays music

accordion: a musical instrument
elegant: stylish

Exercise 3 Understanding the text

Write *T* for true or *F* for false for each statement.

_____ 1. Times Square is near New York City.

_____ 2. Times Square is full of people.

_____ 3. Times Square is international.

_____ 4. Times Square is peaceful.

Exercise 4 Responding to the text

Answer the following questions about the reading.

1. What sounds might you hear in Times Square? _____

   _____

2. Do you agree that people are interesting to watch? Explain. _____

   _____

3. What sentence in the description is the most interesting to you? Why? _____

   _____

Exercise 5 Freewriting

Write for five to ten minutes in your journal. Choose from the topics below or an idea of your own. Don't worry about mistakes.

- Where do you go to watch people? Why?
- Name a city you know. What do you like about it?
- What tourist attractions does your city or country have?
- What time of day is good to visit your city? What time of year? Why?

 In **Writing Process Step 2** you will . . .

- learn to describe places.
- brainstorm ideas and specific vocabulary to use in your writing.
- create an outline for your description.

WRITING TASK Travelers like to learn about a place before they visit. Think about a place that is good for tourists. Describe the place. Go to the Web to use the Online Writing Tutor.

Exercise 1 Brainstorming ideas

A. Work with a partner. Describe each tourist attraction. Which ones do you have where you live?

B. Choose a tourist attraction you know for your topic. It can be one of the pictures or your own idea.

Exercise 2 Brainstorming vocabulary

A. Circle the words that go with the place in bold. Use your dictionary to look up words you do not know.

1. **a museum**	a painting	art	objects	animals	history
2. **a park**	a skyscraper	shade	benches	a lake	ducks
3. **a statue**	horses	walls	a hero	a leader	a soldier
4. **a zoo**	a theater	monkeys	lions	birds	music
5. **a square**	an elevator	a fountain	benches	a monument	gold
6. **an arena**	sports	fans	traffic	seats	a field
7. **a beach**	sand	ocean	waves	mountains	sea birds

B. Select words to describe your topic. Put them in the correct category in the chart.

Singular: Words that have *a* or *an*	Plural: Words that end in –s	Noncount: Words without *a/an* or plural –s
a painting		

Rhetorical Focus

Describing Places
A **description** tells the reader about a place. A description helps the reader make decisions about visiting the place.

Main Idea Sentence
• The main idea sentence introduces the place.

Supporting Detail Sentences
• Supporting details tell where something is.

• Details tell how a place looks.

• Details explain why the place is interesting or important.

Exercise 3 Reading a student paragraph

Read the paragraph. Who or what is El Pípila?

El Pípila

In Guanajuato, Mexico there is an important monument. It is on a hill. There are steps to the top. The monument is a statue of El Pípila. He is a hero of Mexican independence. There is a rock on his back. The rock protects him from bullets. He is strong, and he shows the strength of the Mexican people.

Exercise 4 Examining the student paragraph

A. Answer the questions about the paragraph.

1. Why is El Pípila a hero? _____

   _____

2. How do you know El Pípila is strong? _____

   _____

3. Do you want to see the monument? Why or why not? _____

   _____

B. Examine the organization of the paragraph. Respond to the questions and statements below. Compare your answers with a partner.

1. Circle the topic in the first sentence.

2. Is the first sentence indented? _____

3. How many supporting sentences are there? _____

4. What parts help you know where the monument is? _____

   _____

5. What parts help you know what the monument looks like? _____

   _____

Exercise 5 Making an outline

GO ONLINE

Review your brainstorming ideas and the information on describing places. Then go to the Web to print out an outline template for your paragraph.

 In **Writing Process Step 3** you will . . .

- learn to use prepositional phrases to describe location.
- write a first draft.

Exercise 1 Reading a student paragraph

Read the short paragraph below. Where is the Burj Khalifa?

The Burj Khalifa

The United Arab Emirates has one of the tallest buildings in the world. It is the Burj Khalifa. It is 160 stories high. The height is 828 meters, or 2,716.5 feet. There is an elevator to the top. It is very fast. At the top, visitors see the city of Dubai. They also see the ocean.

Exercise 2 Examining the student paragraph

A. Answer the questions about the paragraph. Use a separate piece of paper.

1. Would you like to see the Burj Khalifa?
2. How do you think people feel when they are at the top?
3. Would you like to live in a tall building like the Burj Khalifa? Explain.
4. What important buildings do you know about?

B. Examine the organization of the paragraph.

1. Circle the topic in the first sentence.
2. Are all the supporting sentences about the topic? _____
3. How many supporting sentences are there? _____
4. Is there at least one subject and one verb in each sentence? _____

GO ONLINE

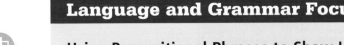
Language and Grammar Focus

Using Prepositional Phrases to Show Location

A **preposition** is a word that allows the writer to tell locations or add other information to a sentence. The preposition is followed by a noun or noun phrase to create a **prepositional phrase.**

   at the top   in the building

Prepositional phrases go after a noun or verb.

   There is a tree **on the hill.**   A path leads **to the tree.**

Sometimes prepositional phrases go at the beginning of a sentence.

   Under the tree, there is a man.

Exercise 3 Identifying prepositional phrases

Underline the prepositional phrases in each sentence.

1. There are benches <u>under the trees</u>.
2. There are lions in the zoo.
3. People relax in a garden near the entrance.
4. Next to the building, there is a fountain.
5. The door to the building is glass.

Exercise 4 Practicing with prepositional phrases

Use the picture to match the sentences on the left with prepositional phrases on the right. Write the new sentences on a separate piece of paper.

STAY OUT OF THE FOUNTAIN

_____ 1. There are birds
_____ 2. The fountain is
__a__ 3. The people are looking
_____ 4. There is a sign
_____ 5. There is a child
_____ 6. There are flowers

    a. at the fountain
    b. in front of the fountain
    c. in the square
    d. in the water
    e. next to the fountain
    f. on top of the fountain

Exercise 5 Writing a first draft

GO ONLINE

Review your notes. Then write your first draft of a description of an important place to visit. Your work should be double-spaced, and it should include the following:

- a title
- margins on both sides
- a main idea sentence
- four or five supporting detail sentences

Go to the Web to use the Online Writing Tutor.

Exercise 6 Peer editing a first draft

A. After writing a first draft, exchange paragraphs with a partner. Use the questions below to give your partner feedback.

GO ONLINE

Peer Editor's Questions

1. What do you like about the topic?

2. Where is the place?

3. What does it look like?

4. Why is it important?

5. What questions do you have about the place?

B. Review your feedback. Make notes for how you will improve your paragraph. Then add, remove, or rewrite information.

 In **Writing Process Step 4** you will . . .

- learn how to edit prepositional phrases.
- learn to use articles and singular and plural nouns with *there is or there are.*
- edit your first draft and write a final draft.

Now that you have written a first draft, it is time to edit. When you edit, you make changes that will improve your writing and correct mistakes.

GO ONLINE

Language and Grammar Focus

Editing Prepositional Phrases

Prepositional phrases are not subjects.

    x In Miami has good beaches. (INCORRECT)

    Miami has good beaches. (CORRECT)

Prepositional phrases do not go between a verb and an object.

    x Tourists enjoy under the trees a cold drink. (INCORRECT)

    Under the trees, tourists enjoy a cold drink. (CORRECT)

    Tourists enjoy a cold drink under the trees. (CORRECT)

Exercise 1 Correcting mistakes with prepositional phrases

Find and correct the mistakes in the sentences below.

1. The water feels ^*cool* in the summer ~~cool~~.

2. We have by the river a park.

3. About Norway tourists travel by ship.

4. The museum has in the garden a statue.

5. In the playground has a climbing wall.

6. People ride in London the subway.

7. There are in the lake boats.

8. In the library has computers.

9. Find in the book the glossary.

GO ONLINE

Language and Grammar Focus

Articles and Singular Nouns with *There is*

Introduce **singular nouns** with the **article** *a* or *an*.

Most nouns begin with a consonant sound. Use *a*.

a building   **a** statue

When a noun begins with a vowel sound (*a, e, i, o, u*), use an.

an arena   **an** island

To introduce a singular noun, it is helpful to use *There is*.

There is a mountain.   **There is** an opening in the mountain.

 Note: The word *the* often goes before singular nouns after they are introduced.

Exercise 2 Practicing with article *a* or *an* and singular nouns

Say the following words out loud. If they begin with a consonant sound, write *a*.
If they begin with a vowel sound, write *an*.

1. _An_ eagle flies.
2. There is _____ door on one side.
3. Seattle has _____ airplane museum.
4. There is _____ path through the trees.
5. People can take _____ tour through the building.
6. There is _____ aquarium with many fish.
7. Visitors might see _____ famous person.
8. There is _____ beach nearby.

GO ONLINE

Language and Grammar Focus

Plural Nouns with *There Are*

Form **plural nouns** by adding an *–s*.

car**s**   street**s**

For nouns that end in *s, z, ch, sh,* and *x,* add *–es*.

beach**es**   glass**es**

For more rules about plurals and spelling, check your dictionary.

GO ONLINE

Some nouns are plural but they do not have *-s*.

Singular	Plural
person	people
child	children
man	men
woman	women

To introduce nouns in the plural form, use *There are*.

There are families in the park.   **There are** children in the water.

Exercise 3 Practicing with plural nouns and *there are*

Rewrite the sentences onto a separate piece of paper. Change the nouns to plural form. Make any other changes necessary.

1. There is a painting by a woman. *There are paintings by women.*
2. There is a hotel nearby.
3. There is a garden outside.
4. There is a bench.
5. There is a person holding a flower.
6. There is a picture of a leader.
7. There is a man selling jewelry.
8. There is a child climbing a tree.

Exercise 4 Editing practice

Read and edit the descriptions. There are five mistakes with singular and plural nouns in each description. Check your answers with a partner.

1. I like to go to Yuldong Park in Korea. There are many thing to see. There is fountain.

   There are interesting sculpture in a garden. For example, there is two big sculptures of ants.

   Peoples like to take pictures of the sculptures.

2. There is market on the water in Thailand. It is near Bangkok. There is people in boats. They

   sell vegetables from their boat. The vegetables are fresh. There are many visitor. They like to

   take picture of the colorful vegetables.

Exercise 5 Editing your work

Review your draft, and look for mistakes. Use the checklist below. Then write a final draft. Go to the Web to use the Online Writing Tutor.

GO ONLINE

Editor's Checklist

Put a check (✓) as appropriate.

CONTENT

○ 1. Do you have a main idea sentence?

○ 2. Do your detail sentences all support the main idea?

LANGUAGE

○ 3. Did you use prepositional phrases to describe places?

○ 4. Did you introduce singular nouns with *a* or *an*?

○ 5. Did you use the correct ending for plural nouns?

○ 6. Did you use *there is* for singular nouns?

○ 7. Did you use *there are* for plural nouns?

○ 8. Did you put periods between sentences?

Go to the Web to print out a peer editor's checklist.

 In **Review** you will . . .

• review using prepositional phrases to describe places.

• practice using the article *a* or *an*.

• review using plural nouns.

• practice editing.

In Putting It All Together you will review what you learned in this unit.

Exercise 1 Identifying prepositional phrases

Underline the prepositional phrases in the sentences below.

1. There is a road beside the mountain.
2. Children play in the sand.
3. Under the sign, there are two doors.
4. The museum is near the park.
5. On the beach, there are shells.

Exercise 2 Practicing with prepositional phrases

Add prepositional phrases to the sentences below.

1. There is an archeology museum.

   There is an archeology museum in the park.

2. The city has a museum.

   _____

3. There are birds.

   _____

4. People enjoy picnics.

   _____

5. Tourists eat lunch.

   _____

Exercise 3 Using the article *a* or *an*

Write *a* or *an* in front of the singular noun in each item below. If the noun is plural, leave it blank.

1. _a_ a. lake   _____ b. rivers   _a_ c. beach   _an_ d. umbrella

2. _____ a. park   _____ b. bench   _____ c. animal   _____ d. swings

3. _____ a. seats   _____ b. field   _____ c. roof   _____ d. advertisements

4. _____ a. street   _____ b. trees   _____ c. view   _____ d. kiosks

Exercise 4 Using plural nouns

Rewrite the sentences with the correct plural form. Use a separate piece of paper.

1. Many person photograph birds.
2. There are family in the park.
3. Tourists wear sunglasss at Kilyos Beach.
4. Childs like the city zoo.
5. There are many bench for visitor.

Exercise 5 Practice editing singular and plural noun mistakes

Correct the mistakes with singular and plural nouns in the sentences below.

1. There are people in a boats.

2. The childs are happy.

3. There is a people inside.

4. There are soldier on horses.

5. There is elevator.

6. There is oranges for sale.

Exercise 6 Correcting a short paragraph

Read and edit the paragraph. There are seven mistakes in grammar and punctuation.

Tourists enjoy visiting in my country a special bazaar The bazaar has roof over it. There is many shops inside people buy at the shops many souvenirs. There are carpets, dish, and other handicrafts.

 In **Timed Writing** you will . . .

• practice writing with a time limit.

Practice your test-taking skills with the following practice topic. Read the prompt. Then follow the steps below.

> There are many ways for a restaurant to be successful. Describe a successful restaurant. Why is it successful?

Step 1 BRAINSTORMING: 2 minutes

Write down ideas and vocabulary.

Step 2 OUTLINING: 3 minutes

Fill in the outline chart with ideas for your writing.

Topic Sentence	
Where is it?	
What does it look like?	
Why is it successful?	
How does the food taste and smell?	

Test-Taking Tip

Leave wide margins, and double-space your work. This will give you room to go back and edit.

Step 3 WRITING: 20 minutes

Use your brainstorming notes and outline to respond to the prompt.

Check for mistakes. Use this checklist.

Editor's Checklist

Put a check (✓) as appropriate.

○ 1. Did you write a main idea sentence to introduce the topic?

○ 2. Did you answer all the questions in your outline?

○ 3. Did you use prepositional phrases to describe places?

○ 4. Did you introduce singular nouns with *there is* and *a* or *an*?

○ 5. Did you introduce plural nouns with *there are* and use the correct plural ending?

○ 6. Did you put a period after each sentence?

Go to the Web to print out a peer editor's worksheet.

Topics for Future Writing

Write a short paragraph on one of these topics.

Education: Describe a well-organized classroom.

Useful Vocabulary
Nouns: bookshelves, desks, maps, cabinets, containers
Adjectives: neat, new, clean, big, labeled

Fine Arts: Describe a painting, photograph, or sculpture.

Useful Vocabulary
Nouns: painting, frame, artwork, bronze, oil paint, watercolor, camera
Adjectives: large, gold, old, modern, thick, soft, natural, strange

Geography: Describe a scenic place in your country.

Useful Vocabulary
Nouns: hills, mountains, valleys, cliffs, beaches, rivers, lakes, deserts
Adjectives: high, sandy, deep, frightening, round, dry, clear

UNIT 3

Describing Objects

Unit Goals

Rhetorical Focus

- describing personal items

Language and Grammar Focus

- adjectives for visual details
- adjectives after *be*
- adjectives before nouns
- first-person simple present

Descriptions of things help readers understand what items look like or why they are important.

Exercise 1 Thinking about the topic

Discuss the pictures with a partner.

- What are the people in the photographs wearing?
- Which person looks intelligent? Why do you think so?
- Which person looks popular?
- How do personal items show someone's personality?

Exercise 2 Reading about the topic

Joseph is a student. He is changing schools. He is worried about the way he looks in glasses. What is his problem with glasses?

September 7

I have **mixed feelings** about my glasses. Do they make me look smart or boring? My glasses cost a lot of money. They are made of wire with square glass lenses. There is a special part in the middle of each lens for reading. These glasses also help me work on the computer and see my friends' expressions clearly. However, I worry that I look like a **nerd**. I look like someone who does not do anything physical. There is nothing bad about reading or computers, but I worry that people will have an opinion about me because of my glasses.

mixed feelings: both good and bad opinions
nerd: a person who is not popular or fashionable and is not good in social situations

Exercise 3 Understanding the text

Write *T* for true or *F* for false for each statement.

_____ 1. Joseph likes everything about his glasses.

_____ 2. The glasses help Joseph read.

_____ 3. The glasses are square.

_____ 4. Joseph hates to read books.

_____ 5. Joseph thinks he is boring.

Exercise 4 Responding to the text

Answer the following questions about the reading.

1. Why does Joseph have mixed feelings? _____

   _____

2. Do you agree that glasses make people look boring? Explain. _____

   _____

3. What do you think when you see someone wearing glasses? _____

   _____

4. How can Joseph solve his problem? _____

   _____

Write for five to ten minutes in your journal. Choose from the topics below or an idea of your own. Don't worry about mistakes.

- Some people collect nice things such as jewelry, scarves, shoes, or furniture. What do you collect? Why?
- When you buy clothing, what is important to you?
- What colors do you like? Why?
- Do you like new (modern) or old (traditional) styles?
- What kind of stores do you like? Why?

 In **Writing Process Step 2** you will . . .

- learn how to describe clothing and personal items.
- brainstorm ideas and specific vocabulary to use in your writing.
- create an outline for your description.

WRITING TASK Personal items show a lot about people's personalities. Describe one thing that you have that shows your style. It can be clothing or an accessory such as jewelry or a scarf, or it can be sports equipment or something in your home. What does the item say about you? Go to the Web to use the Online Writing Tutor.

Exercise 1 Brainstorming ideas

Fill in the chart with two possible topics. Choose one topic for your assignment.

	Something You Wear	Something in Your Home
What words describe it?		
What words describe your feelings about it?		

Look at the pictures. In the spaces below, write words that describe each picture. Choose from the word lists or use your own words.

Picture A: My Backpack	Picture B: My Purse
Vocabulary:	Vocabulary:

Color: black, brown, red, purple, green, gold, silver, blue, white
Size: bulky, compact, roomy, small
Shape: square, round, long
Style: elegant, modern, traditional, casual, stripes, design
Material: plastic, leather, silk, wool, metal, glass
Features: pockets, buckles, snaps, zippers, straps, logo

Rhetorical Focus

Describing Personal Items
A description gives information about an object. Good descriptions help readers understand what an object looks like without actually seeing it.

Main Idea Sentence
• The main idea sentence introduces the object in a general way.

Supporting Detail Sentences
• The supporting sentences give details that help the reader see how something is different from others of the same type.

• Details tell the size, shape, color, and material of the object.

• Details may also give information to help the reader understand the object. For example, they may show what the object says about the writer.

Read the main idea and supporting details. What is a soccer jersey?

My Favorite Soccer Jersey

I collect soccer jerseys, and I wear them almost every day. My favorite team is Barcelona, so I like my Barcelona jersey best. The shirt has short sleeves. It is a smooth material, so it is comfortable. It has red and blue stripes. They go up and down. There is gold writing across the front. There is a club logo on the chest.

A. Answer the following questions about the paragraph. Use a separate piece of paper.

1. Why does the writer like the Barcelona jersey?
2. What three colors does the jersey have?
3. Can you imagine how the jersey looks?
4. Do you think the jersey shows something about the writer's personality?

B. Examine the organization of the paragraph. Respond to the questions and statements below. Compare your answers with a partner.

1. Circle the topic in the first sentence.

2. Is the first sentence indented? _____

3. How many supporting sentences are there? _____

4. What descriptive words help you "see" the topic?`_____

GO ONLINE

Review your brainstorming ideas and the information on describing personal items. Then go to the Web to print out an outline template for your paragraph.

 In **Writing Process Step 3** you will . . .

- learn to use visual details to describe merchandise.
- write a first draft.

Exercise 1 **Reading a student paragraph**

Read the short paragraph below. What makes these slippers special?

The Point of My Slippers

My slippers are in a traditional Moroccan style. They are brown leather on the bottom and sides. The slippers are gold and blue on top. The slippers have a point at the toe. Because of this point, they are different from slippers in other countries.

Exercise 2 **Examining the student paragraph**

A. Answer the following questions. Use a separate piece of paper.

1. What do you learn about the material?
2. What do you learn about the color?
3. Do you think the slippers look nice? What details help you decide?

B. Examine the organization of the paragraph. Respond to the questions and statements below. Then compare your answers with a partner.

1. Circle the topic in the first sentence.

2. Are all the supporting sentences about the topic? _____

3. How many supporting sentences are there? _____

4. Does each sentence begin with a capital letter and end with a period? _____

GO ONLINE

Language and Grammar Focus

Using Adjectives to Add Visual Details
Visual details give specific information about the color, size, shape, weight, fabric, or cost of an item. Without this information, it is hard to know what the shirt looks like in the example below.

I have a nice shirt.

Now look at the sentence with **adjectives.** The adjectives give specific facts that help the reader "see" the shirt.

I have a **dress** shirt. It is **blue.** The shirt has **long** sleeves.

Exercise 3 Practicing using adjectives to write visual details

Look at the pictures below. Then practice using adjectives to write supporting details.

1. **Main idea sentence:** My mother gave me a necklace for my birthday.

   Supporting details: It has a silver chain. The beads are green and blue.

   _____

2. **Main idea sentence:** My watch is simple.

   Supporting details: _____

   _____

3. **Main idea sentence:** I have real cowboy boots.

   Supporting details: _____

   _____

Exercise 4 Writing a first draft

GO ONLINE

Review your notes. Write your first draft of a description of something that you own. Your work should be double-spaced, and it should include the following:

- a title
- a main idea sentence
- margins on both sides
- four or five supporting detail sentences

Go to the Web to use the Online Writing Tutor.

Exercise 5 Peer editing a first draft

A. After writing a first draft, exchange paragraphs with a partner. Use the questions below to give your partner feedback.

GO ONLINE

Peer Editor's Questions

1. What do you like best about the paragraph?

2. Why is the topic important to the writer?

3. What do you learn about the writer's personality?

4. What information helps you picture the item in your mind?

5. What questions do you have about the topic?

Go to the Web to print out a peer editor's worksheet.

B. Review your feedback. Make notes for how you will improve your paragraph. Then add, remove, or rewrite information.

 In **Writing Process Step 4** you will . . .

- learn how to use adjectives with *be*.
- learn to place adjectives before nouns.
- learn to use the simple present with *I*.
- edit your writing and write a final draft.

Now that you have written a first draft, it is time to edit. When you edit, you make changes that will improve your writing and correct mistakes.

GO ONLINE

Language and Grammar Focus

Adjectives after *Be*

Use adjectives after *be* (*is, am, are*) to describe the subject.

My coat is **pretty.**
My boots are **dark brown.***

To form a negative sentence, use *not* after *be.*

My wallet **is not** heavy.

*Adjectives do not change with the plural form.

Exercise 1 Practicing with adjectives after *be*

Unscramble the sentences below. Write the correct sentence on the line.

1. white / my / curtains / are

   My curtains are white.
   _____

2. is / the / jacket / black

   _____

3. metal / buttons / the / are

   _____

4. are / the / gold / earrings

   _____

5. blue / dark / my / is / dress

   _____

6. hat / my / brown / is

   _____

7. striped / tie / is / my

   _____

Language and Grammar Focus

Adjectives before Nouns

Use adjectives before the nouns they describe.

Adjectives with nouns can appear at the beginning of the sentence.

> The **front rooms** are for guests.

Adjectives with nouns can appear after forms of *be*.

> There are **comfortable** slippers by the door.

Adjectives with nouns can appear after verbs.

> I own a **silk scarf**.

Exercise 2 Practicing with adjectives before nouns

Rewrite the sentences below with the adjective in parentheses.

1. There are pictures on the shelves. (beautiful) *There are beautiful pictures on the shelves.*

2. I have a sweater. (green) _____

3. There are flowers on the table. (fresh) _____

   _____

4. My uniform has buttons. (gold) _____

   _____

5. I wear jackets in the winter. (warm) _____

   _____

6. Two mirrors hang in the living room. (large) _____

   _____

Exercise 3 Checking for mistakes with adjectives

Correct the mistakes with adjectives.

1. I need bigs closets.
2. There are plants green on the porch.
3. The carpets are blacks and reds.
4. I like shoes comfortables.
5. The phone has a cover blue.

GO ONLINE

Language and Grammar Focus

The Simple Present in the First Person

When describing an item, use the simple present to describe likes, dislikes, and facts. When *I* is the subject, use the base form of the verb to make statements.

I **like** blue jeans.   I **have** many photographs of my neighborhood.

Use *do not* before the base form to make negative statements.

I **do not like** dark rooms.

Exercise 4 Practicing with singular subjects in the present

Answer the questions below using complete statements.

1. Do you like modern furniture? _No, I do not like modern furniture. I like_
   traditional furniture.

2. What colors do you like? _____

   _____

3. What kind of watch do you own? _____

   _____

4. How many suitcases do you have? _____

   _____

5. Do you wear a uniform? _____

   _____

Exercise 5 Correct mistakes with simple present verbs and *be*

Find and correct the mistakes below.

1. There ~~have~~ *are* buttons on the front.   4. The sides have black.

2. My watch have comfortable.   5. I am not like silver jewelry.

3. I am not have a big car.   6. There have numbers on the side.

Read and edit the descriptions. There are five mistakes with adjectives, verbs, and/or *be* in each description. Check your answers with a partner.

1. There are rose bushes in my yard. They grow next to the door. They not have pretty leaves. They do not tall. Only the roses are beautifuls. Some roses are reds. Other roses is white. They have a smell nice.

2. I have a book about gardens differents. There are pictures colorful of gardens. The gardens are all over the world. Japanese gardens are simples. An English garden has many flowers pretty. A garden Brazilian is full of tropical plants.

Review your draft, and look for mistakes. Use the checklist below. Then write a final draft. Go to the Web to use the Online Writing Tutor.

GO ONLINE

Editor's Checklist

Put a check (✓) as appropriate.

CONTENT

○ 1. Did you introduce the topic with a main idea sentence?

○ 2. Do the detail sentences tell about how the item looks?

○ 3. Do the details describe what the item tells about you?

LANGUAGE

○ 4. Did you use adjectives in the correct order and form to describe nouns?

○ 5. Did you use the correct form of the verb after *I*?

Go to the Web to print out a peer editor's checklist.

 In **Review** you will . . .

• review using visual details and adjectives before nouns.

• practice using the simple present with the first person.

• practice editing.

In Putting It All Together you will review what you learned in this unit.

Exercise 1 **Adding visual details to sentences**

Rewrite the sentences below. Add one adjective to each sentence.

1. There are two letters on the table. _____

   _____

2. I have hair. _____

   _____

3. I do not eat soup. _____

   _____

4. There is a road up the mountain. _____

   _____

5. We love the sky. _____

   _____

6. The morning is a good time to study. _____

   _____

Exercise 2 **Identifying visual details**

Read the main idea sentences below. Put a check (✓) next to visual supporting details. If the details are not visual, leave it blank.

1. My walking shoes are ugly.

   ___✓___ a. The leather is scratched.

   _____ b. I do not like them.

   ___✓___ c. They are dirty.

2. My sofa is modern.

   _____ a. It has a metal frame.

   _____ b. It is big.

   _____ c. My mother gave it to me.

3. There is a lovely ficus tree in my living room.

_____ a. It has bright green leaves.

_____ b. It is between the window and the sofa.

_____ c. It needs a lot of water.

4. I love my winter scarf.

_____ a. It is warm.

_____ b. It is gray.

_____ c. It has white stripes.

5. My ring is expensive.

_____ a. The ring is made of gold.

_____ b. There is a diamond in the middle.

_____ c. It costs a lot of money.

Exercise 3 Practicing the simple present with the first person

Write a sentence saying whether you like or do not like each item below.

1. strong cheese: _____

2. big cities: _____

3. rainy days: _____

4. dogs: _____

5. math: _____

Exercise 4 Editing a paragraph

Read and edit the paragraph. There are five mistakes.

I live in a city rainy. People use umbrellas. Most people have blacks umbrellas. I not like black umbrellas. They are too sad. I have an umbrella red. I also have boots reds. I am happy to walk in the rain.

 In **Timed Writing** you will . . .

• practice writing with a time limit.

Practice your test-taking skills with the following practice topic.
Read the prompt. Then follow the steps below.

> Describe a popular gift for a friend or a family member. Use
> details and examples in your answer.

Step 1 **BRAINSTORMING:** 2 minutes

Write down ideas and vocabulary.

Step 2 **OUTLINING:** 3 minutes

Fill in the outline chart with ideas for your writing.

Topic Sentence _____		
Words that describe size and shape	Words that describe material	Words that describe color

Step 3 **WRITING:** 20 minutes

Use your brainstorming notes and outline to respond to the prompt.

Step 4   **EDITING:** 5 minutes

Check for mistakes. Use this checklist.

GO ONLINE

Editor's Checklist

Put a check (✓) as appropriate.

○ 1. Do your adjectives help readers "see" the gift?

○ 2. Are your adjectives after forms of *be* or before the nouns they describe?

○ 3. Did you use the simple form of verbs after *I*?

Go to the Web to print out a peer editor's worksheet.

Topics for Future Writing

Write a short paragraph on one of the following topics.

Horticulture: Describe a plant.

Useful Vocabulary
Nouns: stem, leaves, buds, petals, branches, roots, thorns
Adjectives: slender, wide, soft, sharp, fragrant, leafy

Interior Design: Describe how a room in your home is decorated.

Useful Vocabulary
Nouns: rug, vase, display, symbol, portrait, arrangement
Adjectives: hand-made, clear, pale, solid, light, bright

Law Enforcement: Describe a police officer's uniform.

Useful Vocabulary
Nouns: fabric, belt, cap, badge, gear
Adjectives: serious, brass, official, dark, heavy

UNIT 4

Explaining Tasks

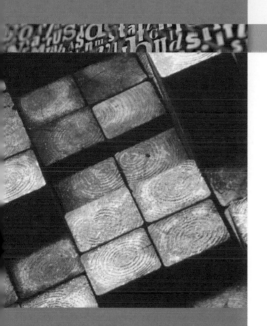

Unit Goals

Rhetorical Focus

- explaining tasks

Language and Grammar Focus

- third-person simple present
- infinitives used to express necessity
- subject-verb agreement
- simple sentences with multiple verbs

Writing Process Step 1 | Stimulating Ideas

When you describe tasks, use a variety of verbs to show actions and functions.

Exercise 1 **Thinking about the topic**

Discuss the pictures with a partner.

- What are the differences between the two robots in the photographs?
- What do you think a human-shaped robot is good for?
- What do you think the insect-shaped robot is good for?
- How many jobs can you name that robots do?

Reading about the topic

The paragraphs below are about a robot called RHex. You saw a photograph of RHex at the beginning of this unit. Which photo is RHex?

Search and Rescue Robots

Engineers and biologists working together have created an interesting new robot called RHex. RHex is the size of a small dog, but it has six legs like an insect. The six legs keep RHex **stable**. RHex moves quickly and does not fall. It also climbs over **obstacles** and up stairs. RHex even swims.

The little robot looks funny, but it does many useful things. RHex helps to find people after an earthquake. It takes photographs of dangerous areas in chemical plants. It climbs into small places to look for problems in factories. Because it can go places that humans cannot, RHex is very important for keeping people safe.

stable: standing firmly
obstacles: any items blocking one's way or stopping progress

Exercise 3 **Understanding the text**

Write *T* for true or *F* for false for each statement.

_____ 1. Biologists and engineers worked together to create RHex.

_____ 2. RHex is the size of an insect.

_____ 3. RHex runs on four legs like a dog.

_____ 4. RHex goes into dangerous places.

Exercise 4 **Responding to the text**

Answer the following questions about the reading.

1. How does RHex's design help it move? _____

   _____

2. What useful tasks can RHex do to help people? _____

   _____

Exercise 5 **Freewriting**

Write for five to ten minutes in your journal. Choose from the topics below or an idea of your own. Don't worry about mistakes.

- What is your favorite software?
- What technology is new in your lifetime?
- Do you use technology in your work? Explain.
- What job is interesting to you. Why?
- What technology do you use to communicate with people? Why?

 In **Writing Process Step 2** you will . . .

- learn to describe a task that people do using technology.
- brainstorm ideas and specific vocabulary to use in your writing.
- create an outline for your explanation.

WRITING TASK Computers and other technologies allow people to do many different jobs. What is a job that requires technology? What does the worker do? Go to the Web to use the Online Writing Tutor.

Exercise 1 Brainstorming ideas

Complete the web with the job titles of people who use technology in their work. Add information about the tasks that they do.

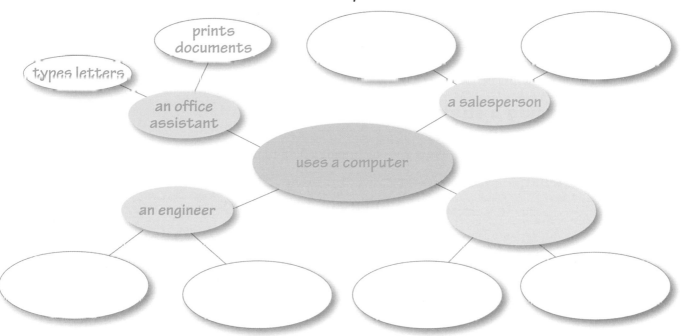

Exercise 2 Brainstorming vocabulary

Fill in the chart with the following verb phrases. Some can be used more than once.

counts money	emails customers	studies bank accounts
sells products	keeps records	takes (someone's) temperature
diagnoses patients	makes phone calls	uses software

a medical professional	
an engineer	
an accountant	
a business person	

Explaining Tasks

Use verbs to describe tasks that people or machines do.

Main Idea Sentence

• The main idea sentence introduces the job title and says something general about the work.

Supporting Detail Sentences

• The supporting sentences explain the tasks.

• Details tell what the person does or what the technology does.

• Details may also give information about what the person/technology does not do.

Exercise 3 Reading a student paragraph

Read the paragraph. How does technology help reporters?

Technology in Journalism

A news reporter uses technology in many ways. He researches stories online with a computer. He also contacts people through the Internet. When he talks to people, he saves their answers on his phone. Then he downloads the information onto a computer. He writes the story and sends it to editors electronically. Sometimes he uses recording technology. He makes a podcast so people can listen to his story on the Internet.

Exercise 4 Examining the student paragraph

A. Answer the following questions about the paragraph.

1. In what ways does technology save time for a reporter? _____ _____

   _____

2. What is different about being a reporter today than in the past? _____

   _____

3. What new technologies help people get news easily? _____

   _____

B. Examine the organization of the paragraph. Respond to the questions and statements below. Compare your answers with a partner.

1. Circle the topic in the first sentence.

2. Is the first sentence indented? _____

3. How many supporting sentences are there? _____

4. Write five verbs that explain a reporter's job. _____

_____

Exercise 5 Making an outline

GO ONLINE

Review your brainstorming ideas and the information on explaining tasks.
Then go to the Web to print out an outline template for your paragraph.

In Writing Process Step 3 you will . . .

- learn to use the simple present with the third person.
- learn about using infinitives to express necessity.
- write a first draft.

Exercise 1 Reading a student paragraph

Read the short paragraph below. Who saves lives with technology?

Saving Lives with Technology

A paramedic uses different kinds of technology in medical emergencies. For example, many people have heart attacks. The paramedic has to treat them quickly. First, she checks the person's heart rate electronically. Then she needs technology to start the patient's heart. A trained emergency medical worker starts a person's heart with a defibrillator.

Exercise 2 Examining the student paragraph

A. Answer the following questions. Use a separate piece of paper.

1. What are two things that a paramedic does to help a heart attack patient?
2. A paramedic needs to be careful. What is another important characteristic?
3. How do you think a paramedic feels after helping a heart attack victim?

B. Examine the organization of the paragraph.

1. Circle the topic in the first sentence.
2. Are all the supporting sentences about the topic? _____
3. How many supporting sentences are there? _____
4. Does each sentence begin with a capital letter and end with a period? _____

Language and Grammar Focus

GO ONLINE

Using Simple Present in the Third Person

To describe tasks that happen regularly, use the **simple present.**

When **third-person** *he*, *she*, or *it* is the subject, add –*s* to the base form of the verb.

An architect **designs** houses.

Use *does not* before the base form to make negative statements.

An architect **does not build** houses.

 *Note: Some verbs are irregular. For example, the verb *have* changes to *has,* and the verb *do* changes to *does* in third-person singular.

Exercise 3 Practicing with third-person singular

Use the subject-verb combinations to write sentences.

1. A gardener / not work inside <u>A gardener does not work inside.</u>

2. A hairstylist / cut hair _____

   _____

3. A businessperson / sell goods and services _____

   _____

4. A medical technician / not prescribe medicine _____

   _____

5. A soccer player / score goals _____

   _____

GO ONLINE

Language and Grammar Focus

Using Infinitives to Express Necessity

To show that something is necessary, use **infinitives** (*to* + verb) after the verbs *have* or *need*. The infinitive does not change.

    A police officer has **to be** careful.   Drivers need **to have** driver's licenses.

In a negative sentence, the person has a choice.

    A city person **does not have to own** a car.

Exercise 4 Using infinitives to express necessity

Rewrite the sentences on a separate piece of paper. Use *have/has* or *need/needs* + an infinitive.

1. An international traveler has a passport. <u>An international traveler has to have a passport.</u>

2. A doctor uses a stethoscope to hear patients' lungs.

3. Photographers do not use film anymore.

4. A bicycle rider does not have a GPS device.

5. The owner charges his cell phone every night.

Exercise 5 Writing a first draft

GO ONLINE

Review your notes. Write your first draft about a job that requires technology. Your work should be double-spaced, and it should include the following:

- a title
- margins on both sides
- a main idea sentence
- four or five supporting detail sentences

Go to the Web to use the Online Writing Tutor.

Exercise 6 Peer editing a first draft

A. After writing a first draft, exchange paragraphs with a partner. Use the questions below to give your partner feedback.

GO ONLINE

> # Peer Editor's Questions
>
> 1. What do you like most about this paragraph?
> 2. What technology does the person use?
> 3. What other technology can you think of for this job?
> 4. What questions do you have about the topic?
>
> **Go to the Web to print out a peer editor's worksheet.**

B. Review your feedback. Make notes for how you will improve your paragraph. Then add, remove, or rewrite information.

 In **Writing Process Step 4** you will . . .

- learn to edit for subject-verb agreement.
- learn how to use more than one verb in a sentence.
- edit your writing and write a final draft.

Now that you have written a first draft, it is time to edit. When you edit, you make changes that will improve your writing and correct mistakes.

GO ONLINE

Language and Grammar Focus

Subject-Verb Agreement in the Simple Present

When the subject is **singular,** add –s to the verb. When the sentence is negative, put *does not* in front of the verb. The verb is in the base form.

A chef **cooks** food.   She **has** kitchen skills.*
A waitperson **does not cook** food.   He **does not have** kitchen skills.

When the subject is **plural,** the verb is in the base form. When the sentence is negative, put *do not* in front of the base form of the verb.

Pilots **fly** planes.   Flight attendants **do not fly** planes.

* Some verbs are irregular. See a dictionary for help with irregular verbs.

Exercise 1 Identifying subject-verb agreement

Create grammatical sentences by writing the correct letter in the blank.

1. __e__ A zookeeper
2. _____ Teachers
3. _____ Accountants
4. _____ A police officer
5. _____ A doctor
6. _____ Software engineers

a. wears a uniform.
b. helps sick people.
c. do not design computer hardware.
d. use a computer to manage money.
e. does not hate animals.
f. write tests.

Exercise 2 Editing subject-verb agreement in sentences

Find and correct the mistakes in the following sentences. Rewrite the sentences on the lines provided.

         does   *design*   *decorates*
1. An interior designer ~~do~~ not ~~designs~~ houses. She ~~decorate~~ rooms.

   An interior designer does not design houses.

   She decorates rooms.

2. Ships carrys products across oceans. They takes a long time.

   _____

   _____

3. A cell phone make life easier for parents. They communicates with their children.

_____

_____

4. The store sell clothing. It do not sell shoes.

_____

_____

5. The robot does not have to breathe. It go places that are not safe for humans.

_____

_____

Exercise 3 Editing for subject-verb agreement

Read and edit the paragraph. There are six more mistakes in subject-verb agreement.

The Science of Finding Oil

uses
A geologist ~~use~~ technology to find oil. He needs to use a special machine. The machine send sound waves into the earth. The sound waves shows a picture. The geologist look at the picture. He do not knows for certain, but he make a guess about the location of oil.

Language and Grammar Focus

Simple Sentences with Two or More Verbs
Some sentences have more than one verb, usually joined by *and*. Both verbs take the same form.

A teacher **explains** grammar and **organizes** activities.
Managers **write** schedules and **make** decisions.

In negative statements, join verbs with *or* and the base form of the verb.

A computer **does not think** or **feel.**
Babies **do not walk** or **talk.**

Exercise 4 Identifying simple sentences with two or more verbs

Underline the subject, and circle two verbs in the sentences below. Write _S_ if the subject is singular. Write _P_ if the subject is plural.

  _P_ 1. Some <u>animals</u> (do not see) or (hear) very well.

  ____ 2. In the fall, leaves change color and fall to the ground.

  ____ 3. A cup of coffee smells good and tastes even better.

  ____ 4. Many city people do not drive or take the bus.

  ____ 5. On holidays, people do not work or travel.

  ____ 6. The tour guide books the hotel and hires a bus.

Exercise 5 Writing sentences with two or more verbs

Complete the sentences below by adding a verb. Make sure the verb has the correct form.

1. A bicycle does not pollute or __occupy__ a lot of space.

2. Taxis pick up passengers and _____ them places.

3. Every morning, children get up and _____ to school.

4. A cook cleans and _____ vegetables.

5. A student reads books and _____ papers.

Exercise 6 Editing sentences with two or more verbs

Read and edit the paragraph. There are four more mistakes with verbs. Check your answers with a partner.

> Some people use technology to make movies. The photographer
> ~~film~~ films the movie. Then an editor looks at the film and make changes.
> Sometimes she doesn't understand or likes the clip. She takes it out
> and put in something else. She also adds music or change the speed.

Review your draft, and look for mistakes. Use the checklist below. Then write a final draft. Go to the Web to use the Online Writing Tutor.

GO ONLINE

Editor's Checklist

Put a check (✓) as appropriate.

CONTENT

○ 1. Did you introduce the topic with a main idea sentence?

○ 2. Do the detail sentences tell what the person does with technology?

LANGUAGE

○ 3. Did you use a variety of verbs?

○ 4. Did you put an -s on verbs with singular subjects?

○ 5. Did you use infinitives after *have* or *need* to show necessity?

○ 6. Did you use two or more verbs in some sentences?

○ 7. Did you check that all verbs are in the correct form?

Go to the Web to print out a peer editor's worksheet.

 In **Review** you will . . .

- review using verbs with singular subjects.
- practice using two verbs in a simple sentence.
- practice editing simple present and infinitives.

In Putting It All Together you will review what you learned in this unit.

Exercise 1 Identifying the correct verb form

Circle the correct form of the verb to complete the sentences below.

1. A police officer (drive / drives) a fast car.
2. A student (work / works) hard in school.
3. A computer (do / does) many things.
4. Waiters (serve / serves) customers.
5. Trees (grow / grows) tall.
6. A child (do not work / does not work).
7. Bicycles (do not use / does not use) gas.
8. A car (have / has) an electrical system.

Exercise 2 Writing sentences with singular subjects

Unscramble the sentences below to create correct sentences.

1. cooks / customers / a chef / for / food _____

   _____

2. flowers / a gardener / grows _____

   _____

3. helps / a nurse / patients _____

   _____

4. customers / not / a teacher / have / does _____

   _____

5. passengers / in / travel / airplanes _____

   _____

6. a child / drive / not / does _____

   _____

7. transports / passengers / a bus driver _____

   _____

Exercise 3 Practicing with two verbs in simple sentences

Use the sentence cues to write sentences with two verbs. Add any words or letters necessary to create the correct form.

1. A traveler / not /eat / or / sleep

_____

2. A baby / eat / and / sleep

_____

3. A store / open / and / close

_____

4. The sun / rise / and / set

_____

5. A bad friend / not / listen / help

_____

Exercise 4 Practice editing simple present and infinitives

Read and edit the paragraph. There are seven mistakes.

> Many people think an actor have an easy life. That is not true.
> An actor work hard. He does not has a steady job. He needs save money
> because he do not always have a job. He goes to auditions for shows.
> He reads the script and answer questions. Directors watch him and other
> actors. Then the actor waits for the directors to decide. Sometimes many
> actors wants the same part.

 In **Timed Writing** you will . . .

• practice writing with a time limit.

Practice your test-taking skills with the following practice topic.
Read the prompt. Then follow the steps below.

> Preparing for a trip is important. Think about a type of
> traveler, such as a tourist or a businessperson. Then describe
> the tasks that person does before a trip.

Step 1 **BRAINSTORMING:** 2 minutes

Write down ideas and vocabulary.

Step 2 **OUTLINING:** 3 minutes

Fill in the outline chart with ideas for your writing.

Type of Traveler	
Verbs that tell what a traveler needs to do	

Step 3 **WRITING:** 20 minutes

Use your brainstorming notes and outline to respond to the prompt.

Test-Taking Tip

Take your test in two parts. First, focus on your ideas when you write. Second, edit your writing for mistakes.

Check for mistakes. Use this checklist.

GO ONLINE

Editor's Checklist

Put a check (✓) as appropriate.

○ 1. Did you write a main idea sentence to introduce the topic?

○ 2. Did you use the ideas, vocabulary, and verbs from your outline?

○ 3. Did you use supporting details to explain what a traveler does?

○ 4. Did you use infinitives after verbs of necessity?

○ 5. Did you use correct subject-verb agreement?

○ 6. Did you use the correct verb form when using more than one verb in a sentence?

Go to the Web to print out a peer editor's worksheet.

Topics for Future Writing

Write a short paragraph on one of the following topics.

Automotive Technology: Describe the functions of one part of a car (for example the battery or the motor).

Useful Vocabulary
Nouns: battery, motor, transmission, carburetor, brake
Adjectives: electrical, mechanical, powerful, heavy
Verbs: carry, connect, provide, remove, replace, check

Cosmetology: Describe the best way to take care of skin or hair.

Useful Vocabulary
Nouns: hairstyle, makeup, cleanser, lotion, sunscreen, conditioner, treatment
Adjectives: dry, rough, smooth, curly, straight, smooth
Verbs: wash, rub, cut, dry, style, apply, color (hair)

Health and Wellness: Describe the habits of a healthy or unhealthy person.

Useful Vocabulary
Nouns: vitamins, nutrition, gym, juice, lifestyle, diet
Adjectives: nutritious, fresh, raw, junk food, sugary, fatty
Verbs: exercise, choose, steam food, prepare, sleep, avoid

UNIT 5 Describing the Past

Academic Focus | Sociology

Unit Goals

Rhetorical Focus

- describing the past

Language and Grammar Focus

- the simple past
- the past with *be*
- spelling rules for verbs in the simple past
- irregular verbs in the simple past
- prepositions of time

In this unit, you will describe a time in the past.

Exercise 1 **Thinking about the topic**

Discuss the picture with a partner.

- Who are the people in the picture?
- Where are they?
- Do you think the picture was taken in the present or in the past?
- How do you think life was different in the past?

An immigrant in the United States remembers the daily routines of his childhood. What routine is he describing?

On Friday mornings, my father woke me up in the dark. I dressed quickly and followed my father out in the first light of the day. The cool air **helped clear our heads** as we walked through the **alleys** to the **public** bathhouse.

The old building had two big rooms. In the first room, we dressed in a towel and waited nervously for our turn. In the second room, bathhouse workers washed us. They used a rough cloth and hot water. They scrubbed us so hard that they took off skin. The bath was painful, but afterwards we **glowed** with **cleanliness**.

helped clear our heads: helped us think clearly
alleys: narrow passages between or behind buildings
public: provided for the use of people in general
glowed: looked good because we were healthy and clean
cleanliness: being clean

Exercise 3 **Understanding the text**

Write *T* for true or *F* for false for each statement.
_____ 1. The writer took baths inside his house.
_____ 2. The writer went to the bathhouse with all of his family.
_____ 3. The bathhouse had two rooms.
_____ 4. The writer bathed alone.

Exercise 4 **Responding to the text**

Answer the following questions about the reading.
1. Why do you think the writer went to a public bathhouse? _____

_____

2. How did the writer feel about the baths? _____

_____

3. How do you think his life is different today? _____

_____

4. Do you think he misses the public bathhouse? How do you know? _____

_____

Write for five to ten minutes in your journal. Choose from the topics below or an idea of your own. Don't worry about mistakes.

- What is something you did ten or more years ago that stays in your memory?
- In what ways was life easier or harder for people in the past?
- In what ways is life easier or harder today?
- Do you think it is good for people to experience a little hardship?
  Why or why not?

 In **Writing Process Step 2** you will . . .

- learn about describing the past.
- brainstorm ideas and specific vocabulary to use in your writing.
- create an outline for your description.

WRITING TASK Many people have clear memories of their past. Describe a family routine or cultural tradition that you remember. Go to the Web to use the Online Writing Tutor.

Exercise 1 Brainstorming ideas

A. Fill in the chart with activities from past memories.

Topic	Memory
Family Gatherings	
Weekend Routines	
Holidays	
Summer Afternoons	
Winter Evenings	
Rainy Days	
Household Jobs	
Other	

B. Choose an activity or routine from your past for your writing.

The chart below introduces verbs in the simple past. Write more words and phrases that can follow the verbs.

	felt did not feel	happy *nervous*
	wanted did not want	to help
	learned did not learn	how to cook quickly
I	expected did not expect	a challenge to find my wallet
	had did not have	to finish by myself
	made did not make	a decision
	left did not leave	the house

Rhetorical Focus

Describing the Past

A **description of the past** gives details about a time and place that may be different from today.

Main Idea Sentence
• The main idea sentence introduces the topic with the time and/or place.

Supporting Detail Sentences
• Supporting detail sentences describe how the person or people lived.

• These sentences tell what people did.

• Details explain what was interesting or important.

Reading a student paragraph

Read the paragraph. Where did the corn come from?

Fresh Corn

When I was younger, I liked to pick corn with my grandfather.
We always went to the field before lunch. The corn was tall. It made
scary noises in the wind, but I felt safe with my grandfather. My
grandfather wore special gloves to protect his hands. He picked corn.
Then we roasted it. The fresh corn tasted sweet.

Examining the student paragraph

A. Answer the following questions. Use a separate piece of paper.

1. What part of the day did the writer choose to write about?
2. What words did the writer use to describe the place?
3. What feelings did the writer experience?

B. Examine the organization of the paragraph.

1. Circle the topic in the first sentence.

2. How many supporting sentences are there? _____

3. Circle the verbs. How many different verbs does the writer use? _____

4. Write the past tense of the following irregular verbs from the text.

   a. go _____   c. feel _____

   b. make _____   d. wear _____

Making an outline

GO ONLINE

**Review your brainstorming ideas and the information on describing the past.
Then go to the Web to print out an outline template for your paragraph.**

 In **Writing Process Step 3** you will . . .

• learn to use the simple past and the simple past of *be*.
• write a first draft.

Read the short paragraph below. Why is the full moon special to the writer?

Full Moon Memory

The night of a full moon was special in my village in Cameroon. The sky was not dark like on other nights. Our parents did not make us sleep. We ran around in the cool blue moonlight. We played games. We laughed. The old people also stayed up. They told stories and enjoyed the night air. Everyone felt happy because the world was beautiful and strange.

A. Answer the following questions. Use a separate piece of paper.

1. What did people do on the night of a full moon?
2. Why is the village night different from a night in a big city?

B. Examine the organization of the paragraph. Respond to the questions and statements below. Compare your answers with a partner.

1. Circle the topic in the first sentence.
2. Are all the supporting sentences about the topic? _____
3. Are all the verbs in the simple past? _____
4. Circle the irregular verbs.

Language and Grammar Focus

GO ONLINE

The Simple Past

Use the **simple past** to give details about something that was true or that happened in the past. There are **regular** and **irregular** forms.

For **regular** verbs add –*ed* to the verb.

> We **laughed**.   She **answered** questions.   I **climbed** the tree.

Irregular past verbs change form. (See page 82 for a list of common forms.)

> go — went   have — had   see — saw

To form the negative, put *did not* in front of the base form of the verb.

> I **did not see** anyone.   She **did not go** with us.

Exercise 3 Identifying regular and irregular past forms

Write *R* for the sentences that have a regular past form. Write *IR* for sentences that are irregular.

_IR_ 1. I fell down.

_____ 2. We made sand houses on the beach.

_____ 3. People celebrated the holidays.

_____ 4. I felt nervous.

_____ 5. We drank sweet tea and ate cake.

_____ 6. We stood on the hill.

Exercise 4 Practicing with verbs in the simple past

Write past sentences. Use the word cues below.

1. They / not have

   They did not have a car.

2. I / carried

   _____

3. She / told

   _____

4. We / not sleep

   _____

5. I / saw

   _____

6. People / not see

   _____

Language and Grammar Focus

GO ONLINE

The Past with *Be*
Be has two forms in the past: *was* and *were*.

I		You	
He, She	was (not) nice.	We	were (not) cold.
It		They	

Exercise 5 **Practicing with past forms of** *be*

Fill in the blanks with the correct form of *be*.

1. They ___were___ not at home.

2. He _____ strong.

3. We _____ clean.

4. I _____ a student.

5. She _____ always hungry.

6. They _____ not rich.

Exercise 6 **Writing a first draft**

GO ONLINE

Review your notes. Then write your first draft of a description of an event from your childhood. Your work should be double-spaced, and it should include the following:

- a title
- margins on both sides
- a main idea sentence
- four or five supporting detail sentences

Go to the Web to use the Online Writing Tutor.

Exercise 7 **Peer editing a first draft**

A. After writing a first draft, exchange paragraphs with a partner. Use the questions below to give your partner feedback.

GO ONLINE

Peer Editor's Questions

1. What do you like about the topic?

2. Where does the event take place, and who was there?

3. Why is the event special to the writer?

4. What questions do you have about the event?

Go to the Web to print out a peer editor's worksheet.

B. Review your feedback. Make notes for how you will improve your paragraph. Then add, remove, or rewrite information.

 In **Writing Process Step 4** you will . . .

- review irregular forms of the simple past and learn spelling rules.
- learn to use prepositions of time.
- edit your first draft and write a final draft.

Now that you have written a first draft, it is time to edit. When you edit, you make changes that will improve your writing and correct mistakes.

Language and Grammar Focus

Spelling Rules for Editing Verbs in the Simple Past

Add *–ed* to most verbs.

    start — started   laugh — laughed

Add only a *–d* when the base form ends in *e*.

    live — lived   scare — scared

If the base form ends in a consonant + *y*, change the *y* to *i* and add *–ed*.

    try — tried   carry — carried

If the base form of a one-syllable verb ends in a single vowel (*a, e, i, o, u*) + consonant, double the final consonant and add *–ed*.

    stop stopped   plan planned

Do not double the final consonants *x*, *w*, and *y*.

    fix — fixed   snow — snowed   stay — stayed

> **!** For more spelling rules, see *Grammar Sense 1*, or check your dictionary.

Exercise 1 Practicing with regular past verbs

Circle the verbs in the sentences below. Rewrite the sentences in the simple past.

SIMPLE PRESENT TENSE	SIMPLE PAST TENSE
1. She believes me.	She believed me.
2. I try a new place.	
3. We watch a sunset.	
4. They enjoy the rain.	
5. She fixes the computer.	
6. We shop for new clothes.	

Exercise 2 Editing for spelling mistakes with regular past verbs

Find and correct the mistakes in the following sentences.

          carried
1. I ~~carryed~~ my lunch.

2. We liveed near a park.

3. They lookked at the sky.

4. She planed a picnic.

5. I plaied with my friends.

6. We tryed new things.

Language and Grammar Focus

Irregular Verbs in the Simple Past
The following is a chart of irregular past verbs from this unit. If you are not sure how to form the simple past of a verb, look up the word in your dictionary.

PRESENT	PAST	PRESENT	PAST	PRESENT	PAST	PRESENT	PAST
build	built	feel	felt	make	made	sleep	slept
come	came	find	found	run	ran	stand	stood
drink	drank	go	went	see	saw	tell	told
eat	ate	have	had	sit	sat	wake	woke

Exercise 3 Editing practice with verbs in the simple past

Find and correct the mistakes in the texts below.

                                                   had
1. As a child, I enjoyed New Year's Eve in Brazil. We ~~have~~ a big dinner. Afterward, we go to the beach. We walk in the water. (two more mistakes)

2. My grandmother did not wanted to live alone. She lived with us. She always tell us stories before bed. She talked about her childhood in Vera Cruz. (two mistakes)

3. My friends and I played soccer in the rain. We enjoy the challenge. We laugh and make a lot of noise. (three mistakes)

Language and Grammar Focus

Prepositions of Time

Use the following **prepositions** to show time.

in	the spring, summer, fall, winter
	the morning, the afternoon, the evening
on	Mondays, Tuesdays, etc. (Monday morning)
	weekends, holidays, rainy days
at	night, noon
	one o'clock, two o'clock, etc.
	10:00 a.m., 2:00 p.m., etc.

Prepositions of time can go before the subject, after the verb, or after the object. When the prepositional phrase is before the subject, use a comma.

On Sunday evening, we spent time with relatives.

We ate **at eight o'clock.**

He grew tomatoes **in the summer.**

Exercise 4 Practicing with prepositions of time

Rewrite the sentences below. Add a prepositional time phrase from the box above. Think of the best place for the prepositional phrase in the sentence.

1. We got money from our relatives. _On New Year's Day, we got money from_
   our relatives.

2. We watched the stars. _____

   _____

3. We came home for lunch. _____

   _____

4. Everyone woke up. _____

   _____

5. We did not work. _____

   _____

6. We picked fruit. _____

   _____

Exercise 5 Editing for prepositions of time

Find and correct the mistakes in the sentences below.

In t
1. ~~The~~ morning, we went to school.

2. At the afternoon, we met at the soccer field.

3. In the weekdays, we were busy.

4. We returned late in night.

5. She gave us hot soup on the evening.

6. Holidays, we bought new clothes.

Exercise 6 Editing your work

Review your draft, and look for mistakes. Use the checklist below. Then write a final draft. Go to the Web to use the Online Writing Tutor.

GO ONLINE

Editor's Checklist

Put a check (✓) as appropriate.

CONTENT

○ 1. Did you introduce a tradition or routine in the topic sentence?

○ 2. Did you give details about how people lived?

LANGUAGE

○ 3. Did you use regular simple past verbs?

○ 4. Did you check for spelling mistakes?

○ 5. Did you use irregular past in the correct form?

○ 6. Did you use complete sentences?

Go to the Web to print out a peer editor's worksheet.

 In **Review** you will . . .

- review using verbs in the simple past.
- practice using prepositions of time.
- practice editing.

In Putting It All Together you will review what you learned in this unit.

Exercise 1 Practicing with verbs in the simple past

Complete the sentences below with simple past verbs from this box and your own words.

answered	drank	laughed	sat	visited
ate	drove	liked	saw	watched
believed	enjoyed	lived	shopped	woke
built	expected	made	slept	worked
came	felt	planned	started	
celebrated	found	ran	stood	
cried	had	returned	told	

1. People _____

2. Everyone _____

3. On summer evenings, my parents _____

4. At noon, we _____

5. We often _____

6. In the morning, I _____

7. My sister _____

8. At night, my brothers and sisters _____

Exercise 2 Editing for mistakes in the simple past

Find and correct past tense mistakes in the sentences below.

1. I did not went to school in the summer.
2. We tryed different recipes.
3. They camed back at night.
4. In the afternoons, she made us a snack and tell us a story.
5. I always runned away from the bees.
6. She did not saw us.
7. They were not found us.
8. At noon, we was tired.

Exercise 3 Practicing with prepositions of time

Answer the questions using prepositional phrases with *at, on,* or *in.*

1. When did you visit your grandparents? _____

   _____

2. What time did you eat lunch? _____

   _____

3. What time of year did you start school? _____

   _____

4. When did you do your homework? _____

   _____

5. When did you see your friends? _____

   _____

Exercise 4 Editing a paragraph

Read and edit the paragraph. There are ten mistakes in verb form, grammar, punctuation, and capitalization.

The Sunset

My grandparents lived on a small mountain in Thailand We visited them in the summer and enjoy nature. On the evenings we sitted outside the house in the cool air. We ate seeds and watch the birds. The clouds was gold, pink, orange, and red. My grandfather drink tea. my grandmother made clothes. Then the stars come out. I liked this part of the day.

 In **Timed Writing** you will . . .

• practice writing with a time limit.

Practice your test-taking skills with the following practice topic. Read the prompt. Then follow the steps below.

> Inventions change the way people live. Think of an invention such as computers, phones, or cars. Write a description of what people did before the invention.

Step 1 BRAINSTORMING: 2 minutes

Write down ideas and vocabulary.

Step 2 OUTLINING: 3 minutes

Fill in the outline chart with ideas for your writing.

Topic Sentence _____	
What was the invention?	
What did people do before the invention?	
What did they not do?	

Step 3 WRITING: 20 minutes

Use your brainstorming notes and outline to respond to the prompt.

Test-Taking Tip

It helps to take a break before you edit. When you finish, turn your paper over for a few seconds. Think about something else. Then go back to your paper and look for mistakes.

Check for mistakes. Use this checklist.

GO ONLINE

Editor's Checklist

Put a check (✓) as appropriate.

○ 1. Did you write a main idea sentence to introduce the topic?

○ 2. Did you answer all the questions in your outline?

○ 3. Did you use verbs in the simple past?

○ 4. Did you check the verbs for correct spelling and form?

Go to the Web to print out a peer editor's worksheet.

Topics for Future Writing

Write about one of the following topics.

Business: Think about business communication before the Internet. How did business people communicate with customers?

Useful Vocabulary
Nouns: telephones, letters, bills, stamps, catalogs, mail order
Verbs: send (sent), call (called), write (wrote), pay (paid)

Culinary Arts: Today, people eat a lot of convenience food. What was different about the way your grandparents got and prepared food in the past?

Useful Vocabulary
Nouns: ingredients, appliances, produce, ovens, knives, jars
Verbs: prepare (prepared), keep (kept), serve (served), boil (boiled), chop (chopped), store (stored)

Education: What was different about student life before computers and the Internet?

Useful Vocabulary
Nouns: blackboards, chalk, typewriters, rulers, calculators
Verbs: search (searched), type (typed), spend time (spent time)

UNIT 6 Explaining Changes

Unit Goals

Rhetorical Focus

* explaining changes with examples

Language and Grammar Focus

* the present continuous
* spelling rules for the present continuous
* conjunctions
* nouns with *the*

Writing Process Step 1 | Stimulating Ideas

In this unit, you will describe and give examples of how a city is changing.

Exercise 1 Thinking about the topic

Discuss the picture with a partner.

- Describe the picture. What is the weather like?
- What kind of bad weather does your city or town have?
- How does your city protect people from bad weather?

Exercise 2 Reading about the topic

Read about the American city Chicago. How is it changing?

Chicago Prepares for the Future

Chicago is famous for its icy winds. However, climate scientists believe that one day Chicago will have a different kind of bad weather. They expect the city to have a warmer and wetter climate by 2100. This hotter climate will create new problems, so city leaders are making changes now.

When they build new schools, builders add air-conditioning. When they repair streets, they use a special kind of **pavement**. The new pavement lets water **seep** through. It prevents **flooding**. Builders are also planting more southern variety trees. The trees help stop flooding, and they provide shade. The shade lowers the temperature.

pavement: the hard surface of a road or sidewalk
seep: flow very slowly through something
flooding: when an area is covered with water, especially from rain

Exercise 3 Understanding the text

Write *T* for true or *F* for false for each statement.

_____ 1. Scientists believe that Chicago will be hot in the future.

_____ 2. City leaders want to stop changes in the weather.

_____ 3. Traditional paved streets can create flooding.

_____ 4. Chicago will have more trees in the future.

Exercise 4 Responding to the text

Answer the following questions about the reading. Use a separate piece of paper.

1. Why is Chicago changing?

2. Do you agree that Chicago needs to make these changes now? Explain.

3. In what other ways will the changes help Chicago?

Exercise 5 Freewriting

Write for five to ten minutes in your journal. Choose from the topics below or an idea of your own. Don't worry about mistakes.

- What kinds of weather do you experience where you live?
- What was your city like 20 years ago?
- What problems does your city have?
- What do you like about your city?
- What is changing in your city?

 In **Writing Process Step 2** you will . . .

- learn to explain with examples.
- brainstorm ideas and specific vocabulary to use in your writing.
- create an outline for your explanation.

WRITING TASK Cities are always changing. In this unit you will write about something (a neighborhood, district, or street, for example) that is changing in your city or town. How is it changing? Give examples to support your observations. Go to the Web to use the Online Writing Tutor.

Exercise 1 **Brainstorming ideas**

Fill in the diagram with notes about changes in your city or town.

Notes

Increasing

Past

Decreasing

Exercise 2 **Brainstorming vocabulary**

Write an additional example for each box below.

City leaders are . . .

modernizing	spending money on	creating	planting	developing
hospitals airports	public safety	business districts	roses	public transportation

tearing down	getting rid of	supporting	repairing	planning
old houses	traffic	pedestrians	bridges	new neighborhoods

Rhetorical Focus

Explaining Changes with Examples

To explain changes, introduce a specific change. Then give examples to show how the change is happening.

Main Idea Sentence

• The main idea sentence introduces the change.

Supporting Detail Sentences

• Supporting details tell where the change is happening.

• Details give reasons why and/or how the change is happening.

• Supporting detail sentences give examples.

Exercise 3 Reading a student paragraph

Read the paragraph. What is positive about the change?

Getting around Seoul

Transportation in Korea is changing. City leaders in Seoul are solving traffic problems. For example, the city is using smart traffic lights. The smart lights change to green when a lot of cars are waiting. The government is also spending money on public transportation. The city has a modern and fast new train system.

Exercise 4 Examining the student paragraph

A. Answer the following questions about the paragraph.

1. What change does the writer focus on? _____

_____

2. One example of a change is smart lights. What is the other example? _____

_____

3. Do you think it is a good idea for a city to spend money to improve transportation?

Why or why not? _____

_____

B. Examine the organization of the paragraph. Respond to the questions and statements below. Compare your answers with a partner.

1. Circle the topic in the first sentence.

2. How many supporting sentences are there? _____

3. How does the writer introduce the first example? _____

4. The writer uses the subject **city leaders** in one sentence. What is another subject that means the same thing or something similar?

_____

Exercise 5 Making an outline

GO ONLINE

Review your brainstorming ideas and the information on explaining changes with examples. Then go to the Web to print out an outline template for your paragraph.

 In **Writing Process Step 3** you will . . .

- learn to use the present continuous.
- write a first draft.

Exercise 1 Reading a student paragraph

Read the short paragraph below. What is changing in the neighborhood?

A Change on Majmar Street

Majmar Street in Esfahan is changing. The neighborhood is very old, and it has narrow alleys. Cars cannot drive in the alleys, so the city is widening the streets. For example, many people are tearing down old houses. They want to build modern three-story buildings. When they tear down an old house, they have to give three meters of land to the city. Then the city widens the street.

Exercise 2 Examining the student paragraph

A. Answer the following questions about the paragraph.

1. What change does the writer focus on? _____
   _____

2. How is the city getting land? _____
   _____

3. What is good and bad about the change? _____
   _____

4. Do you think people like the plan? _____
   _____

B. Examine the organization of the paragraph. Respond to the questions and statements below. Compare your answers with a partner.

1. Circle the topic in the first sentence.

2. Are all the supporting sentences about the topic? _____

3. How many examples are there? _____

4. Is the paragraph in the past tense or the present tense? _____

GO ONLINE

Language and Grammar Focus

The Present Continuous

Use the **present continuous** to show an action that is in progress. It is often used to show that something started before now at an indefinite time and continues.

The present continuous is formed with the present tense of *be* + verb + *–ing*.

They **are coming.**   It **is raining** in London.

To form the negative, put *not* between *be* and the verb + *–ing*.

It **is not moving.**

It is possible to join two present continuous verbs with *and* in a simple sentence. Do not repeat the *be* verb.

They **are building** hospitals and **repairing** the roads.

Exercise 3 Practicing with the present continuous

A. Write complete sentences in the present continuous. Use the cues below. Do not forget to put a period at the end of the sentence.

1. The mayor / encourage / new businesses / provide / jobs.

   The mayor is encouraging new businesses and providing jobs.

2. Hospitals / expect / patients _____

   _____

3. A new school / open / in my neighborhood _____

   _____

4. The city / plant / trees / build / parks _____

   _____

5. People / not / work from home. _____

   _____

6. Business people / develop / downtown _____

   _____

B. Exchange papers with a partner. Check your partner's work for the correct use of the present continuous.

Language and Grammar Focus

Verbs Not in the Present Continuous

The following frequently used verbs are not used in the present continuous:

have*   own   believe   want   like   understand   need

 *The verb *Have* can be used in the present continuous when it does not mean "ownership."

Exercise 4 Practicing with the simple present and the present continuous

Circle the two verbs in each sentence below. Then choose one of the verbs to change into the present continuous.

is building

1. The city ~~builds~~ modern houses because people (want) them.

2. I believe that my city becomes more international.

3. City leaders understand that pollution creates a problem.

4. The city repairs the bridge because people like to walk across it.

5. The city has a new subway, so more people take trains to work.

6. The government owns the land, and they build a sports stadium.

Exercise 5 Writing a first draft

GO ONLINE

Review your notes. Then write your first draft about a change in your city. Your work should be double-spaced, and it should include the following:

- a title
- margins on both sides
- a main idea sentence
- four or five supporting detail sentences

Go to the Web to use the Online Writing Tutor.

Exercise 6 Peer editing a first draft

A. After writing a first draft, exchange paragraphs with a partner. Use the questions below to give your partner feedback.

GO ONLINE

Peer Editor's Questions

1. What do you like about the topic?

2. Where is the place?

3. What is changing?

4. Why or how is it changing?

5. What examples does the writer give?

Go to the Web to print out a peer editor's worksheet.

B. Review your feedback. Make notes for how you will improve your paragraph. Then add, remove, or rewrite information.

 In **Writing Process Step 4** you will . . .

- learn spelling rules for forming the present continuous.
- learn to use conjunctions to combine sentences.
- learn to use *the* with specific nouns.
- edit your first draft and write a final draft.

Now that you have written a first draft, it is time to edit. When you edit, you make changes that will improve your writing and correct mistakes.

Language and Grammar Focus

Editing for Spelling Mistakes with the Present Continuous

Follow these rules when you edit your spelling of verbs in the present continuous.

Remove the *e* before adding *–ing* to verbs that end in *e*.

> leave — leaving

When the verb ends in a vowel + consonant, double the consonant.

> plan — planning

Exercise 1 Editing simple present and present continuous sentences

Review the present continuous on page 96. Then find and correct spelling and grammar mistakes in the following sentences.

1. The government is ~~planing~~ *planning* a new hospital.

2. People is walking across the bridge.

3. Houses are becomeing expensive.

4. He is owning his own business.

5. City leaders are solveing transportation problems.

6. Citizens talking about the new airport.

Language and Grammar Focus

Conjunctions

One way to connect two ideas is to use a **conjunction** to join two sentences. Replace the period with a comma, and add a conjunction.

Use *and* to show that two sentences are related.

> The government is creating new jobs, **and** many people are working.

Use *but* to show contrast.

> Monterrey is building new roads, **but** the traffic is getting worse.

Use *so* to show a result.

> Immigrants are moving to Bahrain, **so** the government is building apartments.

Exercise 2 Identifying conjunctions

Circle the conjunction that shows the relationship between the two sentences.

1. I love both cities, (but / and) I like Rio de Janiero best.
2. The old part is on one side of the river, (but / and) the new part is on the other.
3. Young people are leaving the village, (so / but) many houses are empty.
4. Cars are very expensive, (and / so) many people are riding motorcycles.
5. The stairs are long and steep, (and / but) there is an elevator.
6. The river is polluted, (and / but) it is still beautiful.

Exercise 3 Practicing with conjunctions

A. Complete the sentences below.

1. The shops close at noon, and _people go home for a meal._

2. The neighborhood is close to downtown, but _____

3. There are many small shops nearby, so _____

4. The trees provide shade in the summer, and _____

5. There are many farms nearby, so _____

6. The climate is mild, so _____

B. Exchange books with a partner. Check your partner's sentences. Make sure the relationship between the ideas is clear. Then check for mistakes.

Exercise 4 Editing sentences with conjunctions

Read and edit the paragraph. There are six more mistakes in punctuation and capitalization.

My hometown of Barcelona is beautiful, but it is becoming expensive. There are not many apartments available and, prices for housing are high. For example, a simple apartment in the city costs 1 million euros. So many people live far away from the center. Restaurants are also expensive, The chefs in Barcelona are famous so the restaurants are charging more for good food. For example, a fish dinner costs twice as much as last year.

Language and Grammar Focus

Using *The* with Specific Nouns

Use *the* before nouns that are specific, as in these common situations.

Use *the* when a noun is familiar to the reader because the writer has introduced it in a previous sentence or the context makes it clear. For example, there may only be one of something.

> An ancient bazaar is across town. **The** bazaar is 1,000 years old.
> **The** mayor is talking to **the** police about new traffic laws.

Use *the* when a noun is followed by a prepositional phrase that makes it specific.

> **The** people of Anchorage know a lot about cold weather.

Do not use *the* when the nouns have other determiners like *most, some,* or *many,* or possessive adjectives (*my, your, her, his, their, our*).

> **Most** cities have job opportunities.   **His** plan for Zacatecas worked.

Exercise 5 Identifying specific nouns with *the*

Circle *the* in the sentences below. Then underline the prepositional phrase or introduction that makes it specific.

1. He gave a speech, but few people thought (the) speech was successful.
2. They met at the hotel on Carlos Pellegrini Street.
3. Many people lost their homes in the fire on Grand Boulevard.
4. When people move to Boston, they are surprised at how cold the city gets.
5. Copacabana Beach is popular. The beach attracts millions of visitors every year.
6. The schools in Singapore are very clean.

Exercise 6 Practicing with *the*

Add a missing *the* to each sentence below.

1. ⎯ *The* n ⎯ Name of my mother's city is Nagoya, and most of her family still live there.

2. They live in a small town of about 3,000 people, but town is growing quickly.

3. Amsterdam is crowded. Thousands of bicycles move through city every day.

4. There is an ancient castle. Many tourists like to visit castle.

5. Many years ago, people built walls around Cartagena, and walls are still there.

6. There is a beautiful river in Croatia. People have picnics by river.

7. Capital of Spain is Madrid.

Read and edit the paragraph. There are five more mistakes with the present continuous, conjunctions, *the*, and punctuation.

>   *and*
>
> It is fall, ∧ Denver is change. Denver is high up in the mountains so
>
> the fall is beautiful. For example, the trees are becomeing gold and red.
>
> The mornings is cold but not freezing. People are wearing coats, and are
>
> walking quickly.

Exercise 8 **Editing your work**

Review your draft, and look for mistakes. Use the checklist below. Then write a final draft. Go to the Web to use the Online Writing Tutor.

GO ONLINE

Editor's Checklist

Put a check (✓) as appropriate.

CONTENT

   ○ 1. Does your topic sentence introduce the change in your city?

   ○ 2. Do your supporting detail sentences tell where, why, and how the change happened?

LANGUAGE

   ○ 3. Did you use the present continuous to describe changes?

   ○ 4. Did you use conjunctions *and, but,* or *so* to join sentences?

   ○ 5. Did you use *the* with specific nouns?

   ○ 6. Did you check for spelling and punctuation mistakes?

Go to the Web to print out a peer editor's worksheet.

 In **Review** you will . . .

- review using the present continuous.
- practice using conjunctions.
- review using *the* with specific nouns.
- practice editing.

In Putting It All Together you will review what you learned in this unit.

Exercise 1 Practicing with the present continuous

Write sentences about the photograph below. Use the present continuous.

_____

_____

_____

_____

_____

Exercise 2 Practicing with simple present and present continuous

Correct the sentences below. Change one of the verb phrases to the simple present.

1. He is living downtown, so he is understanding the neighborhood.

2. People are believing the mayor because he is helping the city.

3. Older citizens are trying to take care of themselves, but they are needing help.

4. Many citizens are owning homes, and they are taking care of the neighborhood.

5. The taxes are going up, but people are not wanting to move.

Exercise 3 Practicing with conjunctions

A. Match one sentence from each column.

_d_ 1. Houston has many good restaurants.   a. It is hard to have a perfect diet.

____ 2. The weather is hot in the winter.   b. They cause pollution.

____ 3. Most people try to eat healthy food.   c. They share stories about the past year.

____ 4. People visit their friends.   d. Many of them are not expensive.

____ 5. Cars are useful.   e. People go to the beach.

____ 6. Pilots are careful.   f. They do not make many mistakes.

B. On a separate piece of paper, combine the sentences above using conjunctions *and*, *but*, or *so*.

Houston has many good restaurants, and many of them are not expensive.

Exercise 4 Practicing with *the* before specific nouns

Add *the* where it is needed. Write Ø in the blanks where *the* is not needed.

1. In summertime, _____ children in my neighborhood play outside.

2. When people buy a new car, they make sure _____ car gets good mileage.

3. Flooding causes _____ problems, but civil engineers are trying to solve them.

4. Many people like to climb _____ mountains in Pakistan.

5. Actors have an interesting job, but _____ job requires a lot of hard work.

Exercise 5 Practicing with mistake correction

Read and edit the paragraph. There are six mistakes in the present continuous, combining sentences with conjunctions, and specific nouns with *the*.

> City of Santo Domingo is beautiful right now because of the holiday.
> Everyone is busy but they are friendly. People not working so they go
> shopping. Old part of the town has colorful decorations. For example, many
> businesses put up lights or ribbons. Even boats on the water have lights.

 In **Timed Writing** you will . . .

• practice writing with a time limit.

Practice your test-taking skills with the following practice topic. Read the prompt. Then follow the steps below.

> Technology is changing the entertainment industry.
> Write about a change that you see in movies or games.
> Give examples.

Step 1 BRAINSTORMING: 2 minutes

Write down ideas and vocabulary.

Test-Taking Tip

Think about what you know about the topic. Consider your own experiences and observations watching movies or playing games. Then use your background knowledge to create examples.

Step 2 OUTLINING: 3 minutes

Fill in the outline chart with ideas for your writing.

Main Focus of Change _____	
Example	Example

Step 3 WRITING: 20 minutes

Use your brainstorming notes and outline to respond to the prompt on a separate piece of paper.

Step 4 EDITING: 5 minutes

Check for mistakes. Use the checklist below.

GO ONLINE

Editor's Checklist

Put a check (✓) as appropriate.

○ 1. Did you focus on a specific change?

○ 2. Did you include examples to support your ideas?

○ 3. Did you use the present continuous to show changes in progress?

○ 4. Did you use conjunctions to clarify and connect ideas?

○ 5. Did you check spelling and punctuation?

Go to the Web to print out a peer editor's worksheet.

Topics for Future Writing

Write a short paragraph on one of the following topics.

Business: Explain a change in the way companies advertise products. Give examples.
Useful Vocabulary
Nouns: media, email, sponsorships, endorsements, websites, samples
Verbs: endorse, sponsor, attract (attention), advertise, display

Earth Science: Explain changes in the weather where you live.
Useful Vocabulary
Nouns: wind, rain, heat, humidity, temperature, cold, storm, clouds
Verbs: rise, fall, blow, heat, cool, drop

Economics: Think of an item that is going up or down in price. Explain why the price is changing. Give examples.
Useful Vocabulary
Nouns: inflation, deflation, cost, expense, production, price, supply
Verbs: rise, cost, lower, service, produce, supply

7 Narrating a Past Experience

Unit Goals

Rhetorical Focus

- narrating a past experience

Language and Grammar Focus

- past continuous
- combining past continuous and the simple past
- reporting requests, warnings, and directions with infinitives

In this unit, you will write about something that happened to you in the past.

Exercise 1 Thinking about the topic

Discuss the picture with a partner.

- Describe the person in the picture.
- Why is she alone?
- How old does she look?
- What other words can you use to describe her?

Exercise 2 Reading about the topic

In the novel *To Kill a Mockingbird*, the narrator, Scout, is only nine years old, but she has learned something about her neighbor, Boo Radly, and life in general. How does she feel?

To Kill a Mockingbird

Atticus was right. One time he said you never really know a man until you stand in his shoes and walk around in them. Just standing on the Radley porch was enough.

The street lights were **fuzzy** from the fine rain that was falling. As I made my way home, I felt very old, but when I looked at the tip of my nose I could see fine **misty beads,** but looking cross-eyed made me dizzy so I quit. As I made my way home, I thought what a thing to tell Jem tomorrow. He'd be so mad he missed it he wouldn't speak to me for days. As I made my way home, I thought Jem and I would **get grown** but there wasn't much else left for us to learn, except possibly algebra.

Lee, Harper. *To Kill a Mockingbird.* New York: Harper Collins. 1960.

fuzzy: unclear; blurry
misty beads: raindrops formed like small jewels
get grown: grow up

Exercise 3 Understanding the text

Write *T* for true or *F* for false for each statement.

_____ 1. Scout does not agree with Atticus.

_____ 2. Scout walks to her house in the rain.

_____ 3. Jem will be upset because he missed Scout's adventure.

4. Scout knows algebra.

Exercise 4 Responding to the text

Answer the following questions about the reading.

1. How is the weather? _____

2. Do you think Scout is intelligent? How do you know? _____

   _____

3. What does it mean to stand in someone else's shoes? _____

   _____

4. What will happen when Scout tells Jem her story? _____

   _____

Write for five to ten minutes in your journal. Choose from the topics below or
an idea of your own. Don't worry about mistakes.

- Did you ever "walk around in someone else's shoes"?
- What is an important event in your past?
- Who helped you when you were younger? How?
- What change in your life made you feel grown up (adult)?

 In **Writing Process Step 2** you will . . .

- learn how to narrate a past experience.
- brainstorm ideas and specific vocabulary to use in your writing.
- create an outline for your narrative.

WRITING TASK People learn from past experiences. Write about a time when you felt good about doing something difficult. What was it? What did you learn? Go to the Web to use the Online Writing Tutor.

Exercise 1 Brainstorming ideas

A. Fill in the chart below with notes about your past experiences. Write notes about a time when you or someone else . . .

did something brave.	
were (was) honest.	
helped someone.	
got in trouble.	
changed.	

B. Work with a partner. Ask your partner to tell you a story from his or her chart. Ask questions. Then switch roles. Choose one of the stories for your topic.

Exercise 2 Brainstorming vocabulary

A. Circle the words that best answer the questions about your life experiences. If you don't know a word, look it up in your dictionary.

1. How did you feel when you met new people?
   a. enthusiastic   b. shy   c. nervous   d. confident
2. How did you feel about changes in your life?
   a. excited   b. uncomfortable c. adventurous   d. energetic
3. What did you become good at?
   a. athletics   b. schoolwork   c. making friends d. drawing
4. What kinds of things were you afraid of?
   a. getting in debt b. strangers   c. new places   d. big crowds

B. Review the words from part A. Put a check (✓) next to the words that you might use for your own topic.

Narrating a Past Experience

A **narrative** tells a story. The story ends with something the writer learned and/or wants to teach the reader.

Main Idea Sentence

• The main idea sentence introduces the person and the situation.

Supporting Detail Sentences

• The supporting sentences give details about the place and time of the story.
• Details tell who was there, what they saw, and what happened.
• Details tell how the story ended.

Exercise 3 Reading a student paragraph

Read the short paragraph. What was the challenge?

Early Morning Challenge

When I was living in Ho Chi Minh City, I learned to ride a motorcycle. I had my first job, and I needed to ride to work. I was afraid. My brother helped me. He took me on his motorcycle for one week. After a week, he told me to go alone. We woke up early in the morning. The streets were quiet. My brother was watching me. I was afraid, but I put my hand on the gas. I rode the motorcycle. I was proud that day.

Exercise 4 Examining the student paragraph

A. Answer the following questions about the paragraph.

1. What did the writer do that was difficult? _____

   _____

2. How did her brother help her? _____

   _____

3. Why did the writer feel afraid and proud at the same time? _____

   _____

B. Examine the organization of the paragraph. Respond to the questions and statements below. Compare your answers with a partner.

1. Circle the main event in the first sentence.
2. How many supporting sentences are there? _____
3. Are all the supporting sentences about the topic? _____
4. Highlight the capital letter at the beginning of each sentence.

Exercise 5 Making an outline

GO ONLINE

Review your brainstorming ideas and the information on narrating a past experience. Then go to the Web to print out an outline template for your paragraph.

 In **Writing Process Step 3** you will . . .

- learn to use the past continuous to describe things in progress in the past.
- write a first draft.

Writing Process Step 3 | Developing Your Ideas

Reading a student paragraph

Read the short paragraph below. A person with a limp has difficulty walking. How did the writer get a limp?

My Limp

Something scary happened when I was a young man in Pakistan. I was visiting my uncle. He worked as a forest ranger in the jungle. He told me not to go into the jungle because there were dangerous wolves. I did not listen to him, and one day I went in the jungle. I wanted to see the wolves. I was walking, and I heard a strange noise. Three wolves were running at me. I picked up a stick and fought with the wolves. One wolf bit my leg. I escaped, but now I have a limp, so it is hard to walk.

Exercise 2 **Examining the student paragraph**

A. Answer the following questions about the paragraph.

1. What kind of person was the writer when he was young? _____

   _____

2. What did he do that changed his life? _____

   _____

3. Do you think he was sorry he did not listen to his uncle? _____

   _____

4. What do you think he learned? _____

   _____

B. Examine the organization of the paragraph.

1. Read the first sentence again. What words does the writer use to describe the kind of experience he had? _____

2. Are all the supporting sentences about the topic? _____

3. How many supporting sentences are there? _____

4. Highlight the capital letter at the beginning of each sentence.

5. Circle the period at the end of each sentence.

GO ONLINE

Language and Grammar Focus

The Past Continuous

Use the **past continuous** to show an action that was in progress. It often gives background information when it is used with the simple past.

The past continuous is formed with the past tense of *be* + verb + *–ing*.

I **was walking** along the road. Suddenly, I **saw** a bird.

background information
about something in progress

To form the negative, put *not* between *be* and the verb + *–ing*.

We **were not talking.**

Exercise 3 Using past continuous verbs

Use the cues below to write past continuous sentences.

1. He / not / look / us _He was not looking at us._____

2. I / study / exams _____

3. We / make / noise _____

4. My parents / travel _____

5. They / not / watch / TV _____

6. It / rain / hard _____

Exercise 4 Practicing with the past continuous and the simple past

Answer the questions with the past continuous.

1. How were you feeling when you got married? _____

   _I was feeling nervous when I got married._____

2. Where were you living when you got your first job? _____

   _____

3. What was your mother doing the last time you saw her? _____

   _____

4. Where were you shopping the last time you bought something? _____

   _____

Exercise 5 Writing a first draft

GO ONLINE

Review your notes. Write your first draft about an experience from your past. Your work should be double-spaced, and it should include the following:

- a title
- margins on both sides
- a main idea sentence
- four or five supporting detail sentences

Go to the Web to use the Online Writing Tutor.

Exercise 6 Peer editing a first draft

A. After writing a first draft, exchange paragraphs with a partner. Use the questions below to give your partner feedback.

GO ONLINE

> ## Peer Editor's Questions
>
> 1. What did you like most about the paragraph?
> 2. Where was the writer, and what did the writer do?
> 3. What made the experience interesting for the writer?
> 4. What questions do you have about the topic?
>
> **Go to the Web to print out a peer editor's worksheet.**

B. Review your feedback. Make notes for how you will improve your paragraph. Then add, remove, or rewrite information.

 In **Writing Process Step 4** you will . . .

- learn to use *when* to combine the past continuous with the simple past.
- learn to report requests, warnings, and directions with infinitives.
- edit your first draft and write a final draft.

Now that you have written a first draft, it is time to edit. When you edit, you make changes that will improve your writing and correct mistakes.

Language and Grammar Focus

Combining Past Continuous and Simple Past Sentences with *When*

Use *when* to show that a different action started or interrupted something in progress. The action in progress can go before or after the *when* clause* with no change in meaning. When it goes before, it is followed by a **comma.**

> I was trying to open my umbrella **when** the wind blew it away.

> **When** I found Raul, he was sitting high up in a tree.

> *A clause is like a sentence because it has a subject and a verb. Some sentences have one clause. Some sentences have two or more clauses.

Exercise 1 Practicing with past continuous and *when*

A. Read the sentences below. Add a comma where necessary.

1. When I left, they were talking about the storm.
2. We were picking fruit when something bad happened.
3. I was working in a hotel when it happened.
4. When I saw the fish it was jumping in the water.
5. When I left it was raining.

B. Rewrite the sentences from part A by switching the clauses. Remove or add commas as necessary.

1. They were talking about the storm when I left.
2. _____
3. _____
4. _____
5. _____

A. Write the letter of the sentence in the last column that matches the sentence in the first column.

_e_ 1. We were driving on an empty road		**a.**	the teacher called my name.
_____ 2. We were living in Jordan		**b.**	I found a ticket in the aisle.
_____ 3. I was leaving class	**when**	**c.**	I fell off the bike.
_____ 4. My sister was trying to help me		**d.**	I met my best friend.
_____ 5. I was boarding the plane		**e.**	our car broke down.

B. On a separate sheet of paper, combine the sentences above with *when*. Use *when* at the beginning and the end of sentences.

When our car broke down, we were driving on an empty road.

We were driving on an empty road when our car broke down.

Exercise 3 **Correcting mistakes with the past continuous and *when***

Find and correct the mistakes in the sentences below.

1. When I got home, my mother was ~~cried~~. *crying*

2. I was living in Arequipa, when I got my first job.

3. When we leaving the house, we forgot the umbrella.

4. I ate a sandwich when I was choking.

5. The phone rang, we were sleeping.

GO ONLINE

Language and Grammar Focus

Reporting Requests, Warnings, and Directions with Infinitives

Use *asked*, *warned*, or *told* with the **object pronoun** and an **infinitive** *to* + verb to report requests and directions and to give warnings.

　　She asked me **to be** careful.　　He told us **to stay** away from the fire.

To communicate negative ideas, use *not* before the infinitive.

　　They told us **not to look.**

Practicing with infinitives after *asked*, *warned*, and *told*

Unscramble the sentences below to report requests, warnings, and directions.

1. asked / meet / to / I / my brother / us / at the park

   I asked my brother to meet us at the park.

2. me / the pot / Jasmine / warned / to / not / touch

   _____

   _____

3. to / told / the officer / a report / write / me

   _____

   _____

4. asked / we / the bus driver / take / to / us

   _____

   _____

5. be / to / told / quiet / us / they

   _____

   _____

6. not / he / me / to / told / noise / make

   _____

   _____

Editing practice

Read and edit the paragraph. There are five more mistakes with past progressive, punctuation, and infinitives after *asked*, *warned*, and *told*.

             was

When I ^ traveling in Puerto Rico, I ate a lot of mangos. My wife warned me not eat too many mangos. She told me to ate one or two. I did not listen to her. One day, I ate five mangos. When, I was get ready for bed, I felt very sick. My wife laughed at me. She told to me be careful next time.

Review your draft, and look for mistakes. Use the checklist below. Then write a final draft. Go to the Web to use the Online Writing Tutor.

GO ONLINE

Editor's Checklist

Put a check (✓) as appropriate.

CONTENT

○ 1. Did you introduce the situation?

○ 2. Do the detail sentences tell what happened?

○ 3. Did you explain what you learned from the event?

LANGUAGE

○ 4. Did you use the past continuous to give background information?

○ 5. Did you use the simple past in the correct form?

○ 6. Did you use an infinitive after *warned, asked,* or *told*?

○ 7. Did you use commas and periods correctly?

Go to the Web to print out a peer editor's worksheet.

 In **Review** you will . . .

- review using past continuous.
- practice using *when* to give background information.
- review using infinitives after *asked, warned,* and *told*.
- practice editing.

In Putting It All Together you will review what you learned in this unit.

Exercise 1 Practicing with the past continuous

Circle the correct form of *be* for each sentence below.

1. The women (was / were) making tamales.
2. We (was / were) enjoying the warm weather.
3. My husband (was / were) pushing the car.
4. My sister and I (was / were) looking out the window.
5. The books (was / were) getting wet.

Exercise 2 Choosing past continuous or simple past

Change one of the verbs to the past continuous to clarify meaning.

1. I slept when I heard a noise.
2. When my friend found me, I waited for the bus.
3. He worked in construction when he had an accident.
4. I played with friends when I felt something in my hair.
5. When we lived in Egypt, my parents bought a carpet.

Exercise 3 Combining sentences with *when*

Combine two of the sentences below with *when*. Write the new text on a separate piece of paper.

1. One day, I decided to ride my bicycle to school.
   I was leaving the house.
   My pants caught in the wheel.

   One day, I decided to ride my bicycle to school. I was leaving the house

   when my pants caught in the wheel.

2. I was walking down the street.
   I saw my friend.
   She was carrying a bag.

3. It was a beautiful day.
   I was eating breakfast.
   I decided to go outside.

4. My husband told me to go in the house first.
   I went inside.
   My friends were waiting for me.

Exercise 4 Practicing with infinitives after *asked, warned,* and *told*

Answer the questions below with complete sentences.

1. What did your teacher tell you to study? _____

   _____

2. What did your parents warn you not to eat? _____

   _____

3. What did your friends ask you to do? _____

   _____

4. What did you warn your friend not to do? _____

   _____

5. What did you tell your cousin to bring? _____

   _____

Exercise 5 Editing for mistakes

Read and edit the paragraph. There are six mistakes in past forms, infinitives, and punctuation.

When we first came to the United States, my family move from Ohio to Utah. We was driving on the freeway, when I started missing my rosebush. It had beautiful red roses. I asked my husband turn around. He did not want to. I did not saying anything, but I was sad. A few weeks later, I was cleaning my new house when a delivery man was came. He had a strange package. It was my rosebush. It was a gift from my husband.

 In **Timed Writing** you will . . .

- practice writing with a time limit.

Practice your test-taking skills with the following practice topic. Read the prompt. Then follow the steps below.

> Write a narrative paragraph. Tell a story about a time when you learned a new skill. What did you learn? Who did you learn from? Why was this skill important?

Step 1 BRAINSTORMING: 2 minutes

Write down ideas and vocabulary.

Step 2 OUTLINING: 3 minutes

Fill in the outline chart with ideas for your writing.

General Situation	Main Event	Ending
People/Place/Time		
Lesson		

Test-Taking Tip

Think about the verbs you will use. Remember that within a narrative, verbs are in the simple past or past continuous. When you finish, go back through your work, and make sure all the verbs are complete and have the correct ending.

Step 3 WRITING: 20 minutes

Use your brainstorming notes and outline to respond to the prompt.

Check for mistakes. Use this checklist.

GO ONLINE

Editor's Checklist

Put a check (✓) as appropriate.

○ 1. Did you write a topic sentence that tells the people, the place, and the time?

○ 2. Did you give details about the event, how it ended, and why it was important?

○ 3. Did you use the correct format?

○ 4. Did you use simple past and past continuous to tell your story?

○ 5. Did you use an infinitive after *warned*, *asked*, and *told*?

○ 6. Did you use commas and periods correctly?

Go to the Web to print out a peer editor's checklist.

Topics for Future Writing

Write a short paragraph on one of the following topics.

Computer Science: Tell about a problem with a computer.

Useful Vocabulary
Nouns: hard drive, software, program, power, virus
Verbs: try — tried, reboot — rebooted, load — loaded, crash — crashed, freeze — froze
Adjectives: broken, infected, faulty, damaged

History: Tell about something that a hero in your country did.

Useful Vocabulary
Nouns: war, elections, leaders, heroes, victory, patriot
Verbs: fight — fought, win — won, lead — led, change — changed, create — created
Adjectives: brave, strong, heroic, wise, cautious, loyal, patriotic

Medical Science: Tell about a time when you were sick.

Useful Vocabulary
Nouns: ache, disease, virus, infection, nausea, fever
Verbs: rest — rested, take — took (medicine), recover — recovered
Adjectives: hot, dizzy, weak, nauseated, thirsty, feverish

UNIT 8

Explaining Opinions

Unit Goals

Rhetorical Focus

- explaining an opinion

Language and Grammar Focus

- gerunds to describe tasks and activities
- *because* to give reasons
- introducing examples

To explain an opinion, use reasons such as facts, explanations, or examples.

Exercise 1 **Thinking about the topic**

Discuss the picture with a partner.

- What are the people doing?
- Why are they doing it?
- Where are they going after this?
- How do you think they feel?

Read the article. What is the secret benefit of exercise?

The Secret Benefit of Exercise

New research shows that exercise is good for companies. After employees exercise, they do better work, get along with their co-workers, and have better health. They also visit the doctor less often.

People know exercise is good for the body, but it is also good for the brain. For example, jogging for 30 minutes creates special chemicals in the brain. These chemicals improve people's **moods**. After exercising, people feel good. When they go to work, they have better ideas.

For this reason, many companies are putting **fitness centers** in workplaces. They know that when employees exercise, everyone benefits.

moods: feelings at a particular time
fitness centers: places to exercise and build health

Exercise 3 **Understanding the text**

Write *T* for true or *F* for false for each statement.

_____ 1. Exercise makes employees better workers.

_____ 2. Exercise is good for the body, but it does not affect the brain.

_____ 3. Creativity changes chemicals in the brain.

_____ 4. Exercise can hurt relationships at work.

_____ 5. Companies do not like spending money on fitness centers.

Exercise 4 **Responding to the text**

Answer the following questions about the reading.

1. Should exercise be part of an employee's workday? Why or why not? _____

_____

2. Does exercise improve a person's mood? How do you know? _____

_____

3. What other benefits might exercise have? _____

_____

Write for five to ten minutes in your journal. Choose from the topics below or an idea of your own. Don't worry about mistakes.

- How do you feel after you exercise?
- Do you play a sport? What sport? What do you like about it?
- Is housework or yard work exercise? Why or why not?
- What other activities are enjoyable?
- What other habits are good for workers?

 In **Writing Process Step 2** you will . . .

- learn to support an opinion with reasons and examples.
- brainstorm ideas and specific vocabulary to use in your writing.
- create an outline to explain an opinion.

Writing Process Step 2 | Brainstorming and Outlining

WRITING TASK Physical activity is an important part of a healthy lifestyle. Write your opinion about a healthy activity that is enjoyable and easy to do. Go to the Web to use the Online Writing Tutor.

Exercise 1 Brainstorming ideas

Answer the questions below to brainstorm ideas. Then circle the type of exercise you will write about for your assignment.

What types of exercise do you do . . .	
inside?	
outside?	
with friends?	
alone?	

Exercise 2 Brainstorming vocabulary

Mix and match the words and phrases to write five sentences on a separate piece of paper. You may use a word or phrase more than once.

SUBJECTS	VERBS	OBJECTS
Jogging Playing soccer (or another sport) Practicing martial arts Dancing Doing housework Gardening (Other)	strengthens energizes contributes to benefits stretches improves	muscles positive relationships a healthy body older people strong lungs the heart

Rhetorical Focus

Explaining an Opinion

To write an **opinion,** state something that you believe to be true. Then give reasons to explain your beliefs.

Main Idea Sentence

• The main idea sentence introduces the opinion.

Supporting Detail Sentences

• The supporting sentences give reasons for the opinion.

• Reasons can include facts and explanations.

• Reasons may also be supported with examples.

Exercise 3 Reading a student paragraph

Read the short paragraph below. What is the exercise mentioned in the title?

Exercise by Accident

Many people enjoy gardening, and it is also good exercise. Gardeners grow beautiful flowers or vegetables in their gardens. At the same time, gardeners build strength. For example, digging a hole strengthens arms and legs. Bending over and pulling weeds stretches muscles. Gardeners get these benefits without leaving their homes or spending money.

Exercise 4 Examining the student paragraph

A. Answer the following questions about the paragraph.

1. Why is exercise in the garden accidental? _____

   _____

2. What kinds of gardening activities are considered to be exercise? _____

   _____

3. Why might gardening be good for older people? _____

   _____

4. In what other ways can people get accidental exercise? _____

   _____

B. Examine the organization of the paragraph. Respond to the questions and statements below. Compare your answers with a partner.

1. Circle the topic in the first sentence.

2. How many supporting sentences are there? _____

3. What examples make it easier to understand the writer's opinion?

   _____

   _____

GO ONLINE

Exercise 5 Making an outline

Review your brainstorming ideas and the information on explaining an opinion. Then go to the Web to print out an outline template for your paragraph.

 In **Writing Process Step 3** you will . . .

- learn to use gerunds to describe activities.
- write a first draft.

Writing Process Step 3 | Developing Your Ideas

Exercise 1 Reading a student paragraph

Read the short paragraph below. Why is karate the perfect exercise?

The Perfect Exercise

Karate is good for teaching many things. For example, it strengthens the mind. Clear thinking is an important skill in karate. People learn to focus before they do something. Karate also strengthens the body. Karate exercises muscles in the back, arms, and legs. When people practice a lot, they also have stronger hearts and lungs.

Exercise 2 Examining the student paragraph

A. Answer the following questions about the paragraph.

1. Why does the writer think karate is good exercise? _____

   _____

2. In what ways is karate good for the brain? _____

   _____

3. Do you agree that karate is good? Why or why not? _____

   _____

4. Can you think of other benefits from practicing karate? _____

   _____

B. Examine the organization of the paragraph. Respond to the questions and statements below. Then compare your answers with a partner.

1. Circle the topic in the first sentence.

2. How many supporting examples are there? _____

3. What tense does the writer use? _____

4. What word comes after the preposition *for* in the topic sentence? _____

Language and Grammar Focus

Using Gerunds to Describe Tasks and Activities

To use a verb as a noun, turn it into a **gerund** by adding *–ing* to the verb.

verb	gerund
walk	walking

Walking is good exercise.

A gerund, like a noun, is used as a subject, object, or object of a preposition.

Jogging strengthens legs. *(subject position)*

Many people enjoy **golfing.** *(object position)**

Some people get exercise by **walking.** *(object of a preposition)*

Many gerunds are followed by nouns to form a gerund phrase.

Playing tennis is a difficult workout.

 Not all objects of verbs are gerunds. Infinitives (*to* + verb) are more common.

Exercise 3 **Using gerund phrases**

**Look at the sentences below. Make a gerund phrase for each bold word.
Use gerunds from the box. More than one answer may be possible.**

cleaning	climbing	doing	learning
lifting	playing	practicing	riding

lifting
1. Many people become stronger from ∧**weights**.

2. Many young people are interested in **gymnastics**.

3. **Soccer** motivates people to exercise often.

4. People benefit from **housework**.

5. In my country, many people enjoy **mountains**.

6. **A bicycle** is good for health and transportation.

Exercise 4 Practicing with gerunds

Fill in the blanks with gerunds or gerund phrases to complete the sentences.

1. Austrians look forward to _____skiing_____ in the winter.

2. In my country, many people enjoy _____.

3. _____ brings people together.

4. In the summer, people get exercise by _____.

5. _____ is good for the heart and lungs.

Exercise 5 Writing a first draft

GO ONLINE

Review your notes. Write your first draft about an exercise that is good for people. Your work should be double-spaced, and it should include the following:

- a title
- margins on both sides

- a main idea sentence
- four or five supporting detail sentences

Go to the Web to use the Online Writing Tutor.

Exercise 6 Peer editing a first draft

GO ONLINE

A. After writing a first draft, exchange paragraphs with a partner. Use the questions below to give your partner feedback.

> # Peer Editor's Questions
>
> 1. Why is the exercise easy and/or enjoyable?
>
> 2. What kinds of examples support the writer's ideas?
>
> 3. What types of people might benefit from this type of exercise?
>
> 4. What questions do you have about the topic?
>
> **Go to the Web to print out a peer editor's worksheet.**

B. Review your feedback. Make notes for how you will improve your paragraph. Then add, remove, or rewrite information.

 In **Writing Process Step 4** you will . . .

- learn about using *because* to give reasons.
- learn language for introducing examples.
- edit your first draft and write a final draft.

Now that you have written a first draft, it is time to edit. When you edit, you make changes that will improve your writing and correct mistakes.

Language and Grammar Focus

Using *Because* to Give Reasons
Use the word *because* to give a reason for an action.

People exercise **because** <u>they want to be healthy</u>.

Because and the reason form a **dependent clause.** The dependent clause goes before or after a main clause. When it goes before, it is followed by a comma.

Many people do not belong to a gym **because joining a gym costs money.**
Because joining a gym costs money, many people do not belong to a gym.

Exercise 1 Editing sentences with *because*

Add a comma, a subject, and/or a verb to correct the sentences below.

1. Because sitting at a desk is not healthy, many office workers ∧poor health.
   have

2. Because sailing is expensive only a few people do it.

3. Tai chi is popular in cities because is easy to do in parks or homes.

4. Because they walk up hills every day country people stay healthy.

5. Because people's bodies need a lot of water, is important to drink water often.

6. Players wear helmets because the sport dangerous.

7. Because many workers take the stairs instead of the elevator they have stronger legs.

8. Many people eat vegetables because nutritious food.

9. Laws require people to wear seat belts because prevent injuries.

Exercise 2 **Practicing with** *because*

Complete the sentences below with your own words.

1. It is hard for people to exercise because _____ *they are busy.* _____

2. People do not have to go outside to exercise because _____

   _____

3. Because vegetables do not have a lot of fat, _____

   _____

4. Getting plenty of sleep is important because _____

   _____

5. Because children have a lot of energy, _____

   _____

GO ONLINE

Language and Grammar Focus

Editing for Mistakes with Gerunds

Do not forget to add *–ing* to the verb when . . .

- the verb is a subject.

   x   Ride a motorcycle is dangerous. (INCORRECT)

   Riding a motorcycle is dangerous. (CORRECT)

- the verb follows a preposition.

   x   People need to dress warmly for ski. (INCORRECT)

   People need to dress warmly for skiing. (CORRECT)

Do not use a gerund after certain verbs that take infinitives. Many of these indicate the future (*plan, hope, expect, want, need, prepare*).

   x   Students expect working hard. (INCORRECT)

   Students expect to work hard. (CORRECT)

Exercise 3 Editing for mistakes with gerunds

Find and correct the mistakes with gerunds in the sentences below.

1. ~~Be~~ *Being* patient is an important characteristic for a nurse.

2. People save money by look for sales.

3. Cook at home helps people eat healthier food.

4. Some doctors approve of take vitamins. Other doctors do not.

5. Write is not easy at first.

6. People often try play sports.

Language and Grammar Focus

Introducing Examples

To introduce an example in the form of a sentence, use *For example,* at the beginning of the sentence.

> In Taiwan, people eat protein for breakfast. **For example**, we might eat a fried egg in a bun.

To introduce an example as a phrase (not a complete sentence), use *such as*.

> Healthy people choose healthy foods **such as** broccoli and carrots.

Exercise 4 Practicing with *for example* versus *such as*

A. Write *C* if the sentence is correct. Write *X* if it is not correct.

__X__ 1. When people go to restaurants and grocery stores, they use apps to get nutritional information for example fat content.

_____ 2. There are many water sports in Maine such as canoeing and fishing.

_____ 3. It is best to choose brightly colored fruits for example purple grapes or green kiwi fruit.

_____ 4. Doctors advise doing something calm before sleeping. For example, they suggest spending ten minutes reading a book.

_____ 5. Avoid foods that contain caffeine such as coffee, tea, and chocolate.

_____ 6. There are a variety of careers in wellness. Such as, a coach, a nutritionist, or a physical therapist can help people stay healthy.

B. Correct the sentences that have an *X*. Use a separate piece of paper. Check your answers with a partner.

Exercise 5 Editing a paragraph

Read and edit the paragraph. There are six more mistakes with *because*, gerunds, punctuation, and giving examples with *for example* and *such as*.

Many healthy habits are simple. ~~Such as~~ ^{For example,} drinking water has many benefits. Because the human body is 60 percent water people need water for keep organs healthy. Water also gives energy. Instead of drink coffee or soda, people should choose water, because does not have sugar. Sugar gives energy, but it also makes people thirsty. Finally, people who do not like water can get it in food for example soup and fruit.

Exercise 6 Editing your work

GO ONLINE

Review your draft, and look for mistakes. Use the checklist below. Then write a final draft. Go to the Web to use the Online Writing Tutor.

Editor's Checklist

Put a check (✓) as appropriate.

CONTENT

○ 1. Did you introduce your opinion in the main idea sentence?

○ 2. Did you give reasons and examples to support your opinion?

LANGUAGE

○ 3. Did you use gerunds to describe activities?

○ 4. Did you use *because* correctly to explain reasons?

○ 5. Did you check for correct punctuation?

Go to the Web to print out a peer editor's worksheet.

 In **Review** you will . . .

- review using gerunds to describe activities.
- review giving reasons and examples.
- practice editing.

Review | Putting It All Together

In Putting It All Together you will review what you learned in this unit.

Exercise 1 Using gerunds to describe activities

A. Fill in the chart with gerunds that describe activities for each box.

At School	At Home	In the City
taking tests		
learning math		
studying		
On Weekends	**During Vacations**	**In the Morning**
With Grandparents	**With Friends**	**With Classmates**

B. Complete the sentences below with gerunds and gerund phrases from the chart in A.

1. _Taking tests_ _____ at school makes me nervous.

2. Most grandparents enjoy _____

3. _____ is my favorite thing to do with friends.

4. My classmates and I help each other by _____

5. When vacation time is near, people look forward to _____

6. _____ downtown makes me nervous.

7. On weekends, my husband and I enjoy _____

Exercise 2 Giving reasons with *because*

Complete the sentences below with an action or a reason.

1. _____ because most jobs require math skills.

2. Many people move from the country to the city because _____
_____

3. _____ because they have to study a lot.

4. A lot of people get sick in the winter because _____

Exercise 3 Practicing with examples using *for example* and *such as*

Complete the sentences below with complete sentences or phrases. Use a separate piece of paper.

1. Many people like fruit such as _____

2. There are many good jobs in construction such as _____

3. In my city, there are many places to shop. For example, _____

4. People can do many things with a smart phone. For example, _____

Exercise 4 Editing for mistakes

Read and edit the paragraph. There are six mistakes in gerunds, connecting sentences with *because*, and examples with *for example* and *such as*

Play soccer is an excellent way to stay in shape. Most young men enjoy play the sport because is a social activity. They can play with their friends. Soccer is also good for strengthen the body. Run for two hours is good for different parts of the body for example the heart and lungs.

 In **Timed Writing** you will . . .

• practice writing with a time limit.

Practice your test-taking skills with the following practice topic.
Read the prompt. Then follow the steps below.

> Many new careers are possible because of changes in the
> economy. Think of a good job for students today. Explain
> why it is a good job. Give reasons and examples.

Step 1   BRAINSTORMING: 2 minutes

Write down ideas and vocabulary.

Step 2   OUTLINING: 3 minutes

Fill in the outline chart with ideas for your writing.

Main Idea Sentence		
Explanation	**Benefits**	**Example**

Step 3   WRITING: 20 minutes

Use your brainstorming notes and outline to respond to the prompt.

Test-Taking Tip

Try to think in English when you write. People make more mistakes when they translate from
one language to another during a timed writing.

Check for mistakes. Use this checklist.

GO ONLINE

Editor's Checklist

Put a check (✓) as appropriate.

○ 1. Did you introduce your opinion of the job in the topic sentence?

○ 2. Did you use *because* to give reasons?

○ 3. Did you use *for example* or *such as* to give examples?

○ 4. Did you use gerunds to describe tasks and activities?

○ 5. Did you check for mistakes in grammar and punctuation?

Go to the Web to print out a peer editor's worksheet.

Topics for Future Writing

Write a short paragraph on one of the following topics.

Hotel and Restaurant Management: Give your opinion of a restaurant.

Useful Vocabulary
Nouns: service, atmosphere, waiter, dish, preparation, appearance
Adjectives: friendly, convenient, affordable, fresh, delicious, elegant

Marketing: Give your opinion of a useful phone or tablet application.

Useful Vocabulary
Nouns: device, function, application, program
Adjectives: digital, electronic, user-friendly, practical

Pharmacy: Give your opinion of a helpful medicine.

Useful Vocabulary
Nouns: aspirin, pain reliever, effects, dose, strength, relief
Adjectives: effective, gentle, convenient, popular

Appendices

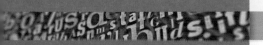

Step 1: Stimulating Ideas

First, make sure you understand the task. Then gather ideas. Think about what you already know about the topic.

▶ **Strategies:** Read your assignment carefully. Talk to classmates about your ideas, and write about them in your journal. Circle the ideas that are the most interesting to you.

Step 2: Brainstorming and Outlining

Make a plan. Organize your main idea and supporting details.

▶ **Strategies:** Make a list, picture, chart, or web. Decide on a main idea. Then put the supporting details in order. Also make a list of vocabulary words that you will use. Finally, make an outline for writing a first draft.

Step 3: Developing Your Ideas

Write a first draft with complete sentences and punctuation. Try to follow the outline as well as you can although you may add new ideas while you write.

▶ **Strategies:** Write your first draft without stopping. Double-space so that you have room to make changes later. When you finish, read your outline and the assignment again. Then read your work. Cross out parts that do not fit. Add new explanations and details. Have a peer read your work and give you feedback.

Step 4: Editing Your Writing

Check your meaning. Did you communicate your ideas clearly? Is your organization easy to follow? Check your grammar, vocabulary, punctuation, and spelling. The final draft should be easy to read with no mistakes.

▶ **Strategies:** Use a checklist to look for mistakes in subject-verb agreement, verb tense, singular/plural forms, word form, word order, and punctuation. Also use a dictionary to check new vocabulary and spelling. Write a final draft. Make sure it has one-inch margins, is double-spaced, has a title, and lists your name, the date, and the class on the top of the first page.

Beginning and Ending a Simple Sentence

A sentence is a complete idea with at least one subject and one verb.

subject	verb		subject	verb

The company <u>hired</u> several engineers. **They** <u>made</u> a plan.

Some sentences have *be* as the verb (*is, am, are, was, were*, etc.).
Bananas **are** healthy. One banana **is** full of vitamins.

Begin a sentence with a capital letter.
The weather was bad that year. **B**ig storms damaged trees.

Use a period to mark the end of a sentence. Put a period immediately after the last letter of the sentence. Leave one space after a period before starting the next sentence with a capital letter.
People are social. **T**hey like to be with other people.

Exercise 1 Editing sentences for capital letters and periods

Edit the sentences below. Add missing periods and capital letters.

1. Maple trees are important. they produce maple syrup.

2. The desert is very hot in the daytime At night, it can be chilly.

3. Tokyo has more than 20 million people most of them live in apartment buildings.

4. Brazil produces coffee. the country also grows sugarcane, corn, and wheat.

5. The city has two famous hotels the Ambassador has a waterfront view. the Commodore faces downtown

Commas with Simple Sentences

Use a comma when introducing a prepositional phrase before the subject.
In St. Petersburg, the summer sun shines at night.

Use a comma after each word in a series. Use *and* before the last word.
Wind, sun, **and** water produce energy.

Do not use a comma when there are only two words or phrases joined by *and*.
Electrical engineers design and repair products.

Exercise 2 Using commas with simple sentences

Add commas where necessary to the sentences below.

1. Oil, natural gas, and coal are fossil fuels.
2. Potatoes, tomatoes and corn come from the Americas.
3. At a checkup nurses weigh patients and give shots.
4. Vocabulary exercises teach nouns, verbs and adjectives.
5. For exercise, my brother swims bikes, and plays tennis.

Using Apostrophes

When a noun is singular, add an apostrophe and -s to show possession.

The store's manager speaks three languages.

When a noun is plural, put the apostrophe after the plural *s*.

The employees' entrance is in the back.

Exercise 3 Identifying singular and plural nouns with apostrophes

Check (✓) the box that correctly identifies the bold noun.

	ONE	TWO OR MORE
1. The **car's** owner lives in England.	✓	
2. The **boys'** school ends in July.		
3. His **brothers'** money disappeared.		
4. The **passenger's** luggage was returned.		

Capitalization

In addition to the first letter of every sentence, capitalize the days of the weeks and the months of the year.

The group meets on the first Tuesday of every month.

Capitalize nouns, verbs, and adjectives in the names of places, people, and organizations.

Mrs. Wang works at The National Aeronautics and Space Administration (NASA) in Washington, D.C.

Exercise 4 Editing capitals

Edit the following texts by adding capital letters where necessary.

1. The university of Pennsylvania is in philadelphia. Classes begin on January 14, and professor howard's sections are on mondays and Wednesdays.

2. The Shinjuku station in tokyo moves nearly 4 million people every day. During the busiest times monday through friday, workers use tools to push people into the trains.

Possessive Adjectives

Use possessive adjectives before a noun to show ownership.

Her phone is like her best friend.

Possessive Adjectives

my	• This is **my** opinion.
your	• **Your** idea is a good one.
his	• **His** company was successful.
her	• The university published **her** book.
our	• **Our** flag has a special meaning.
their*	• They put **their** luggage on a cart.
its	• The company changed **its** name.

*Be careful. It is easy to confuse the spelling with other forms, e.g., *there, they're*

Exercise 5 Practicing with possessive adjectives

Unscramble the sentences below.

1. brought / their / they / children _____

   _____

2. us / our / called / parents _____

   _____

3. sister / her / was / she / texting _____

   _____

4. his / rich / made / idea / him _____

   _____

5. changed / its / the restaurant / menu _____

   _____

Combining Sentences with Conjunctions

Use a comma and a conjunction to show that two sentences are related in some way. The most common conjunctions are *and*, *but*, and *so*.

And joins two similar ideas.
> The students turn in their homework, and the teacher grades it.

But shows a contrast between ideas.
> Ice cream tastes good, **but** it is not healthy.

So tells the relationship between a cause and an effect or a result.
> Traffic was a problem, **so** the city built new roads.

Do not use a comma when you are not joining complete sentences.
> The tour guides hire buses and book hotels.

Exercise 6 Editing sentences with conjunctions

Add a comma when the conjunction joins two sentences.

1. The students write papers but not every week.
2. The stores are open late so people can shop on the way home.
3. A long meal is nice but many people do not have time.
4. Computers have web cams so people can see their families.
5. A doctor works long hours and gets only a few hours of sleep.

Exercise 7 Practicing with conjunctions

Join the two sentences below by writing the correct letter in the blank.

__e__ 1. Tigers like to be alone, but
____ 2. Computer games are fun, so
____ 3. Families need extra space, so
____ 4. Architects design houses, and
____ 5. Televisions are getting bigger, and
____ 6. The beach is busy in the summer, but

a. they move to bigger houses.
b. they are getting more expensive.
c. it is empty in the winter.
d. many children like them.
e. lions live together.
f. construction workers build them.

Run-on Sentences

A run-on sentence is an error. It happens when there is a comma or nothing between two independent sentences.

X Johnny Appleseed is a famous person from history, he planted apple trees across North America. (INCORRECT)

To correct a run-on sentence, use periods between two independent sentences, or add a connector.

Johnny Appleseed is a famous person from history. He planted apple trees across North America. (CORRECT)

Exercise 1 Editing run-on sentences

Edit the texts below to correct the run-on sentences.

1. People need cell phones, <u>they</u> are important for work, people travel away from the
    . They

    office, and they use the cell phone to store information and call customers.

2. Cell phones are important for family life parents use them to check on their children.

3. Cell phones are fun, people read books on cell phones, they also watch movies. Finally, cell phones have games, some of them are for two players.

4. Some parents are worried about their children, they think that kids spend too much time playing games.

5. The signal is good in the metro, people can use their phones on the train.

Fragments

A fragment is an error. It is missing a subject or a verb. Some fragments are dependent clauses. They have a subject and a verb but are not a complete idea.

X The first person in space. (missing verb)
X I like my street. Is changing all the time. (missing subject)
X Many people buy gold. Because it holds value. (dependent clause)

Correct a fragment by adding the missing part of the sentence or by using *and, but,* or *so* to join sentences.

Exercise 2 Editing fragments

Find and correct the fragments and any other mistakes.

1. Credit cards $\wedge$ *are* very useful. When people go shopping. They do not carry money. Carry a credit card.

2. Credit cards are not always good Some people do not use them wisely. When they get the bill. They have to pay a lot of money.

3. When people shop online, they careful.

4. For some people a debit card is better because do not spend too much. When they use a debit card. They only spend money from their bank accounts.

5. Many stores are green. Because people want to save paper. The cashier does not print out the receipt for the customer.

Exercise 3 Editing fragments and run-on sentences

Read and edit the paragraph below. There are five more errors in run-on sentences, punctuation, and capitalization.

There was a fire on Fourth Street last night. *It* it started in the kitchen. As soon as the fire alarm went off. The owner left the house and called the fire department. Before the fire engines arrived, some oxygen tanks exploded. Was a big noise, and the flames spread quickly. The whole house burned down. The owner very sad because the house almost new.

background information Information that helps the reader understand the situation. It can tell where or when something took place, or it can explain why a topic is important.

brainstorm To quickly think of all the ideas and information related to a topic.

controlling idea What the writer is going to say about the topic. The writer might tell a story, give an opinion, or explain the topic in some way.

description What something looks like, sounds like, or other details that help the reader understand what something is and what it is not.

double-spaced Written on every other line so there is a space between lines of writing.

draft To write all the ideas in sentence form for the first time. The writer expects to make improvements to the paper after writing it.

it To review a piece of writing and look for problems meaning or in language.

amples Real situations that explain an idea.

explanation Statements, facts, or circumstances that help the reader understand the writer's ideas. An explanation can have reasons, examples, or definitions.

feedback Comments from a reader that help the writer understand what was good and what was confusing in the writing. Feedback helps the writer know how well the reader understands the ideas.

final draft The finished paper the writer turns in to be published or graded. The writer has fixed the problems so that the draft is clear and there are no errors.

first draft The first time the writer writes ideas on paper. The first draft has the writer's ideas, but they might not be clear, and there might be language errors.

freewriting Writing to explore ideas without worrying about organization or language.

main idea What the writer wants to say in the paper.

margins White space on the right and left sides of the paper. There is no writing in the margins, but a teacher may add comments.

narrative A story that explains something.

opinion What someone believes about something that might be different from what others believe.

organization Making decisions about what ideas will go in a paper and what order they will be in.

outline A plan for what ideas will go into a paper and in what order. An outline does not have a lot of details.

paragraph A piece of writing that introduces an idea and is followed by supporting detail sentences. Usually, a paper has several paragraphs.

peer editing Reading another writer's paper and then discussing the ideas in the paper with the writer. Working with another writer to improve ideas and language in each writer's work.

reasons Explanations that support an opinion. Reasons often answer *why* questions.

revise To improve a piece of writing by adding details, changing details to make them clearer, or taking away ideas that do not fit.

second draft A paper written again after the first draft with improvements to meaning or language.

supporting details Explanations, examples, or definitions that show the writer's ideas in specific ways.

title The name of a paper (also a book, film, or other work). In academic writing, the title is usually a word or phrase that is centered at the top of the first page of the paper.

topic The subject of a piece of writing.

topic sentence A sentence that introduces the subject and tells what the writer will say about that subject.

EFFECTIVE ACADEMIC WRITING INTRODUCTORY BOOK	GRAMMAR SENSE 1
UNIT 1 Subject and Object Pronouns	**CHAPTER 23** Object Pronouns; Direct and Indirect Objects
UNIT 2 Articles Singular Nouns with *There is* Plural Nouns with *There Are*	**CHAPTER 14** Articles **CHAPTER 16** *There Is* and *There Are*
UNIT 3 Adjectives The Simple Present in the First Person	**CHAPTER 6** Descriptive Adjectives **CHAPTER 9** The Simple Present
UNIT 4 The Simple Present in the Third Person Infinitives Used to Express Necessity	**CHAPTER 9** The Simple Present **CHAPTER 24** Infinitives and Gerunds After Verbs
UNIT 5 The Simple Past The Simple Past with *Be*	**CHAPTER 12** The Simple Past **CHAPTER 11** The Simple Past of *Be*
UNIT 6 The Present Continuous Specific Nouns with *The*	**CHAPTER 8** The Present Continuous **CHAPTER 14** Articles
UNIT 7 The Past Continuous Reporting Requests, Warnings, and Directions with Infinitives	**CHAPTER 13** The Past Continuous **CHAPTER 24** Infinitives and Gerunds After Verbs
UNIT 8 Gerunds	**CHAPTER 24** Infinitives and Gerunds After Verbs